IMMORTAL DIAMOND

That Nature Is a Heraclitian Fire and of the Comfort of the Resurrection

 Flesh fade, and mortal trash,
Fall to the residuary worm; world's
wildfire leave but ash;
In a flash, at a trumpet crash,
I am all at once what Christ is, since he
was what I am, and
This Jack, joke, poor potsherd, patch,
matchwood, immortal diamond,
Is immortal diamond.

GERARD MANLEY HOPKINS, S.J.

IMMORTAL DIAMOND

The Search for Our True Self

Richard Rohr

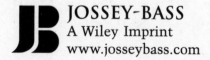

JOSSEY-BASS
A Wiley Imprint
www.josseybass.com

Published by Jossey-Bass
A Wiley Imprint
One Montgomery Street, Suite 1200, San Francisco, CA 94104-4594-www.josseybass.com

Copyright page is continued on page 256.

Library of Congress Cataloging-in-Publication Data

Rohr, Richard.
  Immortal diamond : the search for our true self / Richard Rohr. — 1st ed.
    p. cm.
  Includes bibliographical references and index.   ISBN 978-1-118-30359-7 (cloth);
978-1-118-41978-6 (ebk); 978-1-118-42154-3 (ebk); 978-1-118-43414-7 (ebk)
  1. Self — Religious aspects — Christianity. 2. Identification (Religion) 3. Self-knowledge,
Theory of. 4. Theological anthropology — Christianity. I. Title.
  BT713.R64 2013   233′.5 — dc23

                                                                        2012030242

Printed in the United States of America
FIRST EDITION
HB Printing 10 9 8 7 6 5 4

CONTENTS

> *The fact that life and death are "not two" is extremely difficult to grasp, not because it is so complex, but because it is so simple.*
>
> KEN WILBER

> *We miss the unity of life and death at the very point where our ordinary mind begins to think about it.*
>
> KATHLEEN DOWLING SINGH

In the first aborted ending to Mark's Gospel — the oldest Gospel — the text ends on a very disappointing, and thus likely truthful, note: "They ran away from the tomb frightened out of their wits. They said nothing to a soul, for they were afraid" (16:5–8). What a strange response after having just talked to an angel who told them not to be afraid!

Such running from resurrection has been a prophecy for Christianity, and much of religion, just as in these early Scriptures. I interpret this as the human temptation to run from and deny not just the divine presence, but our own true selves, that is, our souls, our inner destiny, our true identity. Your True

Self is that part of you that knows who you are and whose you are, although largely unconsciously. Your False Self is just who you think you are — but thinking doesn't make it so.

We are made for transcendence and endless horizons, but our small ego usually gets in the way until we become aware of its petty preoccupations and eventually seek a deeper truth. It is like mining for a diamond. We must dig deep; and yet seem reluctant, even afraid, to do so. Note that even the ending that was later added to Mark's Gospel still states three times that the disciples did not believe in the Resurrection (16:11–15). And Jesus "reproached them for their incredulity and their obstinacy" (16:14). This is no high note or happy ending by which to begin a new religion. The first disciples themselves were not the "true believers" that we now try to be. One can only presume it was historically true or they never would have said it this way. (Or maybe it is a recognition that doubt is the necessary partner to real faith.)

The question the three women ask in this first moment of would-be resurrection is still ours: "Who will roll away the rock?" (16:3). Who will help us in this mining operation for True Self? What will it take to find my True Self? How do I even know there is an "immortal diamond" underneath and behind all this rock of my ego, my specific life experience, my own culture? Up to now, it has been common, with little skin off anyone's back, to intellectually argue or religiously believe that Jesus' physical body could really "resurrect." That was much easier than to ask whether *we* could really change or resurrect. It got us off the hook—the hook of growing up, of taking the search for our True Selves seriously.

As many in the Perennial Tradition[1] have said in one way or another, when the "wrong person" uses the right means, even the right means will work in the wrong way. But when the "right person" uses the wrong means, he or she will know how to do midcourse corrections and make it right. I would preferably work with the second person anytime. You must get the "self" right. Otherwise even seemingly good and moral actions will have a tight, stingy, and corrosive character to them. Conversely, the right "self" can even do the wrong thing, and somehow it can always be worked out. You know this from your own experience. We must know who is doing the action and who is doing the reflecting. Is it "your" self? The God self? Or a mere chameleon? That question is foundational to mature spirituality of any stripe.

There is one other thing to take note of here. Mark also says that Jesus "had showed himself *under another form*" (Mark 16:12). Could the radical transformation that resurrection implies be the problem? Is that why so many could not recognize Jesus? I think it is, and it is also our first major clue on our search for the True Self.

We are not so at home with the resurrected form of things despite a yearly springtime, healings in our bodies, the ten thousand forms of newness in every event and every life. The death side of things grabs our imagination and fascinates us as fear and negativity always do, I am sad to say. We have to be taught how to look for anything infinite, positive, or good, which for some reason is much more difficult. We have spent centuries of philosophy trying to solve "the problem of evil," yet I believe the much more confounding and astounding issue is "the problem of good." How do we account for so much gratuitous and sheer goodness in this world? Tackling this problem would achieve much better results.

Somehow resurrection—which I am going to equate with the revelation of our True Selves—is actually a risk and a threat to the world as we have constructed it. After any "raising up" of our True

Selves, we will no longer fit into many groups, even much of religious society, which is often obsessed with and yet indulgent of the False Self, because that is all that it knows.

Whether human beings admit it or not, we are all in love with—even addicted to—the status quo and the past, even when it is killing us. Resurrection offers us a future—dare I say a permanent future—but one that is unknown and thus scary. Humans find it easier to gather their energy around death, pain, and problems than around joy. I know I do. For some sad reason, *it is joy that we hold lightly and victimhood that we grab onto*.

The True Self and its resurrection are always a threat. In the Resurrection of the Christ Body, we are not talking about the resuscitation of an old thing, but the raising up of what will always appear to be an utterly new thing. Resurrection is not about a man returning to his body, nearly as much as *a universal man leading us into a universal future—and doing that by making use of all the past and transforming it* (Ephesians 4:15–16). Note in all the Resurrection accounts in the four Gospels, the marvelous images of running, rushing, excitement, joy, eating, catching a huge harvest, and jumping naked and free into the water. This is all freedom for the future, because the past is over, gone, and totally forgiven.

The clarification and rediscovery of what I am going to call the True Self lays a solid foundation — and a clear initial goal — for all religion. You cannot build any serious spiritual house if you do not first find something solid and foundational to build on — inside yourself. "Like knows like" is the principle. God-in-you already knows, loves, and serves God in everything else. All you can do is fully jump on board. I would call that jump *consciousness*, and I believe the Risen Christ is the icon of full consciousness. In the human mind of Christ, every part of creation knows itself as (1) divinely conceived, (2) beloved of God, (3) crucified, and (4) finally reborn. He carries us across with him, assures us it is okay, and thus models the full journey and final direction of consciousness.[2] That is my major thesis about how Jesus "saves us."

The Perennial Tradition, the mystical tradition that I will be building on here, says that there is a capacity, a similarity, and a desire for divine reality inside all humans. And *what we seek is what we are*, which is exactly why Jesus says that we *will* find it (see Matthew 7:7–8). The Perennial Tradition invariably concludes that you initially cannot see what you are looking for because what you are looking for is doing the looking. God is never an object to be found or possessed as we find other objects, but *the One who shares your own deepest subjectivity*—or your "self." We normally called it our soul. Religion called it "the Divine Indwelling."

I believe the Christ is the archetypal True Self offered to history, where matter and spirit finally operate as one, where divine and human are held in one container, "where there is no distinction between Jew and Greek, slave and free, male and female" (Galatians 3:28). This Christ is going before us into an ever new territory, into "Galilee," which was the forgotten backwater of the Roman Empire and the Jewish religion.

"You are one of *them*! Even your accent gives you away," they say to Peter (Matthew 26:73). "Prophets do not come out of Galilee," say the chief priests (John 7:52). Yet "it is there that you will see him, just as he told you" (Mark 16:7). Perhaps the True Self—and the full Christ Mystery (not the same as organized Christianity)—will always live in the backwaters of any empire and the deep mines of any religion.

Some will think I am arrogantly talking about being "personally divine" and eagerly dismiss this way of talking about resurrection as heresy, arrogance, or pantheism. The Gospel is much more subtle than that. Jesus' life and his risen body say instead that the discovery of our own divine DNA is the only, full, and final meaning of being human. The True Self is neither God nor human. *The True Self is both at the same time, and both are a total gift.*

Such radical newness is threatening, even though it reveals itself in the oldest, truest, and deepest self that we are. Jesus' Resurrection was an absolute refusal to identify with victimhood or create any victims in retaliation. This is an utterly new story line for history. Unlike Lazarus's resurrection (John 11:1–44), Jesus' Resurrection is permanent and definitive for human history. *He is a stand-in for all of us.*

In this excerpt from "They Have Threatened Us with Resurrection" Guatemalan poet Julia Esquivel says what I am grabbing for beautifully:

It is something within us that doesn't let us sleep,
that doesn't let us rest,
that won't stop pounding
deep inside,
it is the silent, warm weeping
of Indian women without their husbands,

it is the sad gaze of children
fixed somewhere beyond memory, . . .

What keeps us from sleeping
is that they have threatened us with Resurrection!
Because every evening
though weary of killings,
an endless inventory since 1954,
yet we go on loving life
and do not accept their death!

. . . because in this marathon of Hope,
there are always others to relieve us
who carry the strength
to reach the finish line
which lies beyond death.

Join us in this vigil
and you will know what is is to dream!
Then you will know how marvelous it is
to live threatened with Resurrection!

To dream awake
to keep watch asleep,
to live while dying,
and to know ourselves already resurrected![3]

Only our True Self can talk this way and mean it. To the False Self—the self driven by ego and its limited concerns—such poetry is surely and merely poetry, a cheap greeting card, forgettable, and a poor attempt to whistle in the dark. But *there is* a True Self, a risen presence, and it is "something here within us which doesn't let us sleep." So let's try now to roll away the rock, clear the debris, and get back to mining for our True Self. You will find a diamond.

Since you do not think yourselves worthy of eternal life, we must now turn to the pagans.
PAUL AND BARNABAS, ACTS 13:46

I am writing this book for secular seekers and thinkers, believers and nonbelievers alike, and that huge disillusioned group in recovery from religion itself. Surprisingly, these are often more ready to see and honor Mystery than many religious people are. I can no longer wait for, or give false comfort to, the many Christians who are forever "deepening their personal relationship" with a very tiny American Jesus—who looks an awful lot like them. I would much prefer to write for those like Jane Fonda, who said recently, "I feel a presence, a reverence humming within me that was, and is, difficult to articulate." Well, Jane, we are going to try to articulate and affirm that *humming* here.

Because far too many religious folks do not seriously pursue this "reverence humming within them," they do not recognize that something within them needs to be deeply trusted and many things must be allowed to die — not because they are bad, but because they perhaps cannot get them where they want to go. Spirituality tends to be more about unlearning than learning. And when the slag and dross are removed, that which evokes reverence is *right there waiting*!

Many religious people seem to think that God, for some utterly unexplainable reason, loves the human past (usually their own group's recent past) instead of the present or the future of this creation. As Jaroslav Pelikan so wisely put it years ago, *"Tradition is the living faith of the dead. Traditionalism is the dead faith of the living, and I suppose I should add, it is tradition- alism that gives Tradition such a bad name."*[1] We can do much better than substituting mere traditionalism for actual God experience.

Our identification of God with the past has done the present and future no favor. Old mistakes are still mistakes, and we do not need to keep repeating them. For much of the world, this preoccupation with the past comes across as a divine approval of everybody else's death (non-Christians, heretics, Native peoples, "sinners," women, the poor, slaves, and on and on), and never our own. Many people have lost all interest in our grand spiritual talk and our Scriptures because they too often have been used by people who are themselves still small (who are stuck in their False Self). It does not help to deny that we are stuck, and yet it does not help to stand arrogantly above it all either—as if we do not all share in the one great human crucifixion of reality, the one "world sorrow" (*Weltschmerz*, the Germans call it). We Christians affirm the communion of saints in the Nicene Creed, but I think there should be an equal belief in the "communion of sinners." We are all fully a part of both groups.

My hope is that this book will above all else clarify for you, and especially confirm in your own experience, a few things that are true for people of any religion or no religion at all. I will use God language, because it is still the language of 95 percent of the world and 99 percent of history, but I think you will agree that what I say about grace, death, and resurrection is true for everybody and does not need specifically religious language at all.

The following three paragraphs came to me very clearly in a very short time while walking along the sea during my Lenten hermitage in 2012. In some ways, they summarize this book at the very beginning:

1.   **The goodness of God fills all the gaps of the universe, without discrimination or preference**. God

is the gratuity of absolutely everything. The space in between everything is not space at all but Spirit. God is the "goodness glue" that holds the dark and light of things together, the free energy that carries all death across the Great Divide and transmutes it into Life. When we say that Christ "paid the debt once and for all," it simply means that God's job is to make up for all deficiencies in the universe. What else would God do? Basically, grace is God's first name, and probably last too. *Grace is what God does to keep all things he has made in love and alive—forever*. Grace is God's official job description. Grace is not something God gives; grace is who God *is*. If we are to believe the primary witnesses, an unexplainable goodness is at work in the universe. (Some of us call this phenomenon God, but that word is not necessary. In fact, sometimes it gets in the way of the experience, because too many have named God something other than Grace.)

2. **Death is not just physical dying, but going to full depth, hitting the bottom, going the distance, beyond where I am in control, fully beyond where I am now**. No wonder it is scary. Death is called "the descent into hell" in the early Christian creeds and in other sources, "the pit," "the dark night," "Sheol," or "Hades." We all die eventually; we have no choice in

the matter. But there are degrees of death before the final physical one. If we are honest, we acknowledge that we are dying throughout our life, and this is what we learn if we are attentive: *grace is found at the depths and in the death of everything.* After these smaller deaths, we know that the only "deadly sin" is to swim on the surface of things, where we never see, find, or desire God and love. This includes even the surface of religion, which might be the worst danger of all. Thus, we must not be afraid of falling, failing, going "down."

3. **When you go into the full depths and death, sometimes even the depths of your sin, you come out the other side—and the word for that is res-urrection**. Something or someone builds a bridge for you, recognizable only from the far side, that carries you willingly, or even partly willing, across. From all that we hear from reputable and reliable sources (mystics, shamans, near-death visitors, and "nearing-death experiences"), no one is more surprised and delighted than the traveler himself or herself. Something or someone seems to fill the tragic gap between death and life, but *only at the point of no return*. None of us crosses over by our own effort or merits, purity, or perfection. We are all carried across by an uncre-ated and unearned grace—from pope, to president,

to princess, to peasant. Worthiness is never the ticket, only deep desire, and the ticket is given in the desiring. The tomb is always finally empty. There are no exceptions to death, and there are no exceptions to grace. And I believe, with good evidence, that there are no exceptions to resurrection.

In this investigation of True Self, False Self, resurrection, and transformation, I will be using all New Testament Gospel accounts, along with Paul and John's letters, and Acts of the Apostles too, but if Scripture is not a natural authority for you, you can ignore the citations! While I hope these spiritual intuitions and ideas will stand on their own apart from the Bible, *I will cite Scripture generously to demonstrate that these are not just my ideas.* I am standing on the Judeo-Christian tradition and in that light will also be quoting scholars, saints, theologians, and poets to get us to the perennial truths that all religions share.

I will be trying to use the three-pronged methodology of Scripture, Tradition, and inner experience, which balance and affirm one another when all three live in mutual honoring and respect. Personal experience for me is the underdeveloped "third something" needed to overcome the tired and dualistic food fight between Catholic "tradition" and Protestant "sola Scriptura." Critical reason is then precisely what it takes to coordinate these three principles in a fair way.[2]

THE APPENDIXES: PRACTICE-BASED EXPERIENCE

Since the eighteenth-century Enlightenment, there has been little emphasis on spiritual practices and pathways wherein you could know holy and true things for yourself. John Wesley, the father of what become the Methodist tradition, tried with his various "methods" and practices to bring people to God, but it does not seem that as many hearts were as "strangely warmed" as his was. We still had our wonderful "contemplative orders" in the Catholic church, but even they had lost the older traditions of the prayer of quiet and "prayer beyond words."[3] Catholics and Orthodox and Anglicans have their sacraments and liturgies, but too often they became rote repetition, often encouraging unconsciousness instead of consciousness, especially among many who were most tied to them. The ego, it seems, will find any way to take over, especially in the dangerous world of religion, and it often does, with the most clever of disguises. As Zen Masters are known to say, "Avoid spirituality if at all possible; it is one insult after another." They know that true religion "insults" your ego and does not give it easy comfort.

Up to now, we have been more driven by outer authority ("It is a sin if you don't" or "The church says . . .") than drawn in by the calm and loving inner authority (the in-dwelling Holy Spirit) of prayer, practice, and inner experience. This has a much better chance of allowing you to meet and know your True Self. For all practical purposes, this change of identity is the major—almost seismic—shift in motivation and consciousness itself that mature religion rightly calls *conversion*. It is the very heart of all religious transformation ("changing forms").[4] Without it, religion is mostly a mere belonging system or a mere belief system, but it does not radically change your consciousness or motivation.

We must return to practice-based spirituality where the vantage point switches *from looking at God to looking out from God*. That will become clear and inviting as the book unfolds, I hope, and in the practices offered in the appendixes at the back of the book. Christianity is much more about living and doing than thinking. As Thomas Aquinas, no Catholic lightweight, put it, *Prius vita quam doctrina* ("Life is prior to doctrines").[5]

Whatever I will try to say in this book, it is for the sake of one thing: life—"life more abundantly" (John 10:10) and life for all groups. Life in multitudinous forms has clearly been given to us from known time—beyond the boundaries of any one religion, any one nation, any one ethnicity, any one time period, and any single ideology. And life is not just the unique possession of humans.

My only job, and yours too, is to imitate God in the same love of life.[6] And if God has given such grace and given life so abundantly and so broadly (Acts 11:22), then who am I to stand in God's way (11:17)? The best any of us can do is to back up what is already and obviously happening. Perfect spirituality is just to imitate God.

IMMORTAL DIAMOND

CHAPTER 1

What Is "The True Self"?

*In this high place
it is as simple as this,
Leave everything you know behind.*

*Step toward the cold surface,
say the old prayer of rough love
and open both arms.*

*Those who come with empty hands
will stare into the lake astonished,
there, in the cold light
reflecting pure snow,*

the true shape of your own face.
    DAVID WHYTE, "TILICHO LAKE"

Conservatives look for absolute truth; liberals look for something "real" and authentic. Spouses look for a marriage that will last " 'til death do us part." Believers look for a God who never fails them; scientists look for a universal theory. They are all on the same quest. We are all looking for an immortal diamond: something utterly reliable, something loyal and true, something we can always depend on, something unforgettable and shining. There is an invitation and an offer for all of these groups from John's very short Second Letter, when he writes: "There is a truth that lives within us that will be with us forever" (2 John 2). But most of us know little about this, so we end up as St. Augustine admits in his *Confessions*: "Late have I loved you, Beauty so very ancient and so ever new. Late have I loved you! You were *within*, but I was *without*."[1]

We give up eventually—or do not even try—to seek this truth and instead retreat into ourselves, as if to say, "I alone will be my reference point." It is the most common problem of individualism and egocentricity. I think they go together. We split and retreat into ourselves, but we invariably go to our ego (small self, the False Self) because that is all we know about. It is the common default position, even if it is largely unconscious. Yet it often takes over, and, depending on the severity of our "splitness," it makes all common forms of life, including marriage, lasting friendships, and most commitments, largely impossible. *But this retreat into the personal ego self is both absolutely right and terribly wrong at the same time.* In this book I hope to demonstrate what makes both of these assertions true.

We are right about going inside; otherwise we become lost in an outer and revolving hall of mirrors, as Augustine confesses above. But the question is, "Which inside?" I am using the language of the True Self and the False Self, which many have found quite helpful in talking about these very points. It is good and necessary to pull back into your True Self, but it is quite a disaster if you pull back into what is your False Self for too long (or, worse, never leave it). Both True Self and False Self will feel like your "self," so you see the confusion. One might be called true "centering," and the other is the more common "ego centering," which shows itself to be the core of the problem.

So Jesus, and most other great spiritual teachers, make it very clear that there is a self that has to be found and one that has to be let go of or even "renounced" (Mark 8:35; Matthew 10:39, 16:25; Luke 9:24; John 12:26). Buddhism allows no compromise or softening of this essential message, which is why many are attracted to its utter honesty.

That there are two selves is rather constant in the Perennial Tradition, although the language might be very different from group to group. The important issue is how we tell the difference. Those who deny a sacred source to the universe ("God") have no way of naming something "true" and must resort to psychology, philosophy, and cultural norms alone to find something authoritative. And they are very good—as far as they go. Those of us who claim to believe in God more often than not deny that "we are already his children" (1 John 3:1) and create arbitrary hoops to jump through—at which few fully succeed if they are honest. So my moral self, which is always in flux, becomes the measure, and we have again lost any Absolute Measure. It seems *the False Self would rather have very few "wins" than let God win with everybody*. This is my sad conclusion after a lifetime of working in many churches on many continents, and it is summed up in an often murdered text by most preachers and translators: "*I am calling all of you, but so few of you allow yourselves to be chosen*" (Matthew 22:14).[2]

We are going to talk about the two selves in many ways. Like Socrates's peripatetic method, we will just keep "walking around" it in this book. The search for soul has gained a bit of clarity in our time by finding words that make sense to the modern, more psychological mind. We might now call the False Self our small self or ego, and we might call the True Self our soul. When the True Self becomes clearer to you, and it will for most of you, you will have grounded your spirituality in its first and fundamental task, and you will have hired the best counseling service possible. I love to tell people, "You have just saved yourself ten thousand dollars in unnecessary therapy!" Why? Because in finding your True Self, you will have found *an absolute reference point that is both utterly within you and utterly beyond you at the very same time.* This grounds the soul in big and reliable truth. "My deepest *me* is God!" St. Catherine of Genoa shouted as she ran through the streets of town, just as Colossians had already shouted to both Jews and pagans, "The mystery is Christ within you—your hope of Glory!" (1:27).

The healthy inner authority of the True Self can now be balanced by a more objective outer authority of Scripture and mature Tradition. Your experience is not just your experience, in other words. That's what tells you that you are not crazy. That God is both utterly beyond me and yet totally within me at the same time is the exquisite balance that most religion seldom achieves, in my opinion. Now the law is written on both tablets of stone (Exodus 31:18) and within your heart (Deuteronomy 29:12–14), and the old covenant has rightly morphed into the new (Jeremiah 31:31–34), just as it was already understood and lived by holy Jews. Jesus fully represents this ideal Jewish balance. Remember, Jesus was not a "Christian"!

People who find this wholeness are balanced in general and tend to flourish, as opposed to either mere conformists or mere rebels who just take sides on everything—with no wisdom required. Think of poor Galileo Galilei who, under pressure from the church to deny that the earth moves around the sun, says quietly before he dies, "And yet it moves!" He wisely knew how to survive in a totalitarian system, and yet now he survives and thrives as the Father of Modern Science and the modern popes have exonerated him. You are both the Body of Christ and only a part of the Body of Christ at the same time. You are both the center of the world and on the edge of that same world, or as St. Bonaventure put it, "the center is now everywhere and the circumference is nowhere."

Your personal experience of chosenness is precisely what allows you to pass on that same experience to others, say both Isaiah and Paul (Isaiah 2:1–5, 56:1–7; Romans 11:16ff.). *Outer spiritual believing* tends to say, "Only here" or "only there," while *authentic inner knowing* tends to say, "Always and everywhere." We start elitist and we end egalitarian. And Ken Wilber rightly adds "Always!" What we receive freely, we give away freely (Matthew 10:8). Outer authority told us we were indeed special (that's the only way to get started), but maturing inner authority allows us to see that everyone is special and unique, although it usually takes the maturity of the second half of life to see this. Young zealots still think it's all about them.[3]

I promise you that the discovery of your True Self will feel like a thousand pounds of weight have fallen from your back. You will no longer have to build, protect, or promote any idealized self image. Living in the True Self is quite simply a much happier existence, even though we never live there a full twenty-four hours a day. But you henceforth have it as a place to always go back to. You have finally discovered the alternative to your False Self. You are like Jacob awakening from sleep and joining the chorus of mystics in every age. "You were here all along, and I never knew it!" he says (Genesis 28:16). He anoints the stone pillow where this happened and names it *Bethel*, or "the house of God and gate of heaven" (28:17–18).[4] Jacob then carries the presence with him wherever he goes. What was first only there is soon everywhere. The gate of heaven is first of all in one concrete place, better if carried with you, and best when found everywhere. That is the progression of the spiritual life.

CLUES AND EVIDENCE

Who of us has not asked, "Who am I?" "Who am I really?" "What am I all about?" "Is there any essential 'me' here?" It is as if we are all a big secret to ourselves and must search for clues, however obscure they may be. Yet the search never stops fascinating us, even as we grow older. (If it does, we have almost certainly stopped growing.) Any lecture or class on understanding yourself always draws great interest, even from otherwise jaded or superficial people.[5] One sees this fascination in little children as their eyes widen if you tell them about the day they were born, or what they were like "as a kid," or what they might "be" when they grow up. Try it, and notice how children quiet and listen with intense interest at almost anything about themselves. They gaze at you with wonder and excitement and invariably want to hear more. These messages must feel like oracles from another world to them and doorways into still-hidden secrets.

This curiosity about ourselves grows more intense in the teen and young adult years as we try on a dozen costumes and roles, and we surely covet any recognition or praise of our most recent incarnation. We quickly grab it and try it on for size, as if to say, "This might be me!" Some never take their costume off. A too early or too successful self becomes a total life agenda, occasionally for good but more often for ill. Think of the many young athletes, musicians, and poets who become obsessed with their identity but never make it to the big time. Even if they do succeed, there are too many stories of unhappiness, being lost, and self-destruction. Our ongoing curiosity about our True Self seems to lessen if we settle into any "successful" role. We have then allowed others to define us from the outside, although we do not realize it. Or perhaps we dress ourselves up on the outside and never get back inside. When I explore the True Self in this book, I am talking about a second dressing up, which will actually feel much more like a dressing down.

This confusion about our True Self and False Self is much of the illusion of the first half of life, although most of us do not experience the problem then.[6] Only later in life can we perhaps join with Thomas Merton, who penned one of my favorite lines, *"If I had a message to my contemporaries it is surely this: Be anything you like, be madmen, drunks, and bastards of every shape and form, but at all costs avoid one thing: success. . . . If you are too obsessed with success, you will forget to live. If you have learned only how to be a success, your life has probably been wasted."*[7] Success is hardly ever your True Self, only your early window dressing. It gives you some momentum for the journey, but it is never the real goal. You do not know that, however. In the moment, it just feels right and good and necessary—and it is. For a short while.

I remember hearing a story, reportedly true, about a young couple putting their newborn in the nursery for the night. Their four-year-old son said to them, "I want to talk to the baby!" They said, "Yes, you can talk to him from now on." But he pressed further, saying, "I want to talk to him now and by myself." Surprised and curious, they let the young boy into the nursery and cupped their ears to the door, wondering what he might be saying. This is what they reportedly heard their boy say to his baby brother: "Quick, tell me where you came from. Quick, tell me who made you? I am beginning to forget!" Could that be true? Have most of us forgotten? Is this what Jesus was referring to when he would often teach that we have to become like little children to "get it"?

Most spirituality has said, in one way or another, that we have all indeed begun to forget, if not fully forgotten, who we are. Universal amnesia seems to be the problem. Religion's job is purely and simply one thing: to tell us, and keep reminding us of who we objectively are. Thus, Catholics keep eating "the Body of Christ" until they know that they *are* what they eat — a human body that is still the eternal Christ. What else would the message be? Avoiding this objective and wonderful message, many clergy have made the Eucharist into a reward for good behavior and missed the core Gospel for the sake of a small contest where they just happen to give out the merit badges. Religion's job is to keep "re-minding" us of what we only know "in part" (1 Corinthians 13:12). This book hopes to remind you of what you know and who you are at your core — and in a way that you can't forget. Then whatever you say or do will come from a good, deep, and spacious place. The True Self always has something good to say. The False Self babbles on, largely about itself.

Is it possible that we do know our True Self at some level? Could we all know from the beginning? Does some part of us know — with a kind of certitude — who we really are? Is the truth hidden within us? Could human life's central task be a matter of consciously discovering and becoming who we already are and what we somehow unconsciously know? I believe so. Life is not a matter of creating a special name for ourselves, but of uncovering the name we have always had. Most Native cultures look for inherent symbols at a child's birth—and that became the child's sacred name. Maybe this is what lovers are doing for one another with their sweet nicknames.

Our True Self is surely the "treasure hidden in the field" that Jesus speaks of. It is your own chunk of the immortal diamond. He says that we should "happily be willing to sell everything to buy that field" (Matthew 13:44)—or that diamond mine! Could any one thing be that valuable that we would sell everything for it? In all the Gospels, Jesus is quoted as saying, "What will it profit you if you gain the whole world and lose your own soul?" (Matthew 16:26), and the context invariably implies he is talking about something happening in *this* world. If you find the treasure hidden in your own field, then everything else comes along with it. It is indeed the "pearl of great price" (Matthew 13:46) to continue our precious gem metaphor.

The early Christian writers tell us that this discovery of our True Self is also at the same time a discovery of God. I have far too often seen the immature and destructive results of people who claim to have found God and do not have even a minimum of self-knowledge. They try to "have" God and hold onto their false and concocted little self too. It does not work (1 John 4:20). I have also met many who appear to know themselves and do at some good levels, but not at the largest and divine level; they have to keep scrambling for private and public significance by themselves and in their mental ego. They still live in a separate and very fragile self.

Some who use the language of integral theory or "spiral dynamics" call it the "mean green" level: these are people who are just smart enough to dismiss everybody below them as stupid and everybody above them as falsely spiritual.[8] A little bit of enlightenment is a very dangerous thing. I have seen it in myself, in many clergy, and especially in the arrogance of many academics, early feminists, and loners who can never trustfully belong to any group and seem to believe they have the only correct ideas. Their "smartness" makes them also mean or arrogant, and we intuitively know this should not be true.

The two encounters with a True God and a True Self are largely experienced simultaneously and grow in parallel fashion. If I can do nothing more in this book than demonstrate why and how this is the case, I will have achieved the best purpose here.

One of Jesus' most revealing one-liners is, "Rejoice only that your name is written in heaven!" (Luke 10:20).[9] If we could fully trust this, it would change our whole life agenda. This discovery will not create overstated or presumptuous individualists, as religion usually fears, but instead makes all posturing and pretending largely unnecessary. Our core anxiety that we are not good enough is resolved from the beginning, and we can stop all our climbing, contending, criticizing, and competing. All "accessorizing" of any small, fragile self henceforth shows itself to be a massive waste of time and energy. Costume jewelry is just that, a small part of an already unnecessary costume.

Most of Christian history has largely put the cart of *requirements* before the "horsepower" itself, thinking that loads of carts, or "I have the best cart," will eventually produce the horse. It never does. *The horsepower is precisely our experience of primal union with God.* Find God, the primary source, and the spring water will forever keep flowing (Ezekiel 47:1–12; John 7:38) naturally. Once you know that, the problem of inferiority, unworthiness, or low self-esteem is resolved from the beginning and at the core. You can then spend your time much more positively, marching in the "triumphal parade" (2 Corinthians 2:14), as Paul so playfully calls it.

You see, the horse does all the work. Your work is of another kind: to stay calmly and happily on the road and not get back into the harness. St. Teresa of Avila used a similar metaphor when she described how you can either keep digging the channel or find the actual spring and let it just flow toward you, in you, and from you. Her entire mystical theology is about finding that Inner Flow and not wasting time digging trenches.

SOUL, OUR INHERENT IDENTITY

My studied conviction is that our inherent identity is what almost all the world religions and philosophies have essentially meant by *soul*. We still have many different definitions for *soul*, which reveals the insight of the original Greek word, where *psyche* (soul) literally meant butterfly. Soul and the True Self have always been hard to pin down; they are elusive and subtle like butterflies. Our inability to see the True Self clearly is like our inability to see air: it is everywhere and so it is nowhere. Thus, learning to pay positive attention is the secret formula of almost all mature religion.[10] Any ideological, angry, or fear-based process will only reinforce the False Self. The ego always has an opportunistic agenda. The soul has no agenda whatsoever except to see what is — *as it is* — and let it teach you. Like a butterfly, it alights, tastes, and then moves forward.

Let me try to capture this butterfly soul in its essence: *your soul is who you are in God and who God is in you.* You can never really lose your soul; you can only fail to realize it, which is indeed the greatest of losses: to have it but not have it (Matthew 16:26). Your essence, your exact "thisness," will never appear again in another incarnation. As Oscar Wilde said, "Be yourself; everyone else is already taken." Your True Self and your soul come from the Manufacturer — "hidden inside the box," as the commercials say.

As you are probably beginning to notice, I seem to equate the soul with the True Self and yet they are also a bit different. In some ways they are interchangeable in the sense of revealing that "eternal" part of you, the part of you that knows the truth. But I must also say that the True Self is probably larger than the soul, because *it includes Spirit and embodiment too.* Both reveal to us the immortal diamond that God has planted within us, and they often operate as one.

You (and every other created thing) begins with a divine DNA, an inner destiny as it were, an absolute core that knows the truth about you, a blueprint tucked away in the cellar of your being, an *imago Dei* that begs to be allowed, to be fulfilled, and to show itself. As it says in Romans (5.5), "It is the Holy Spirit poured into your heart, and it has been given to you."

Your True Self is what makes you, you. It is like the Risen Presence that "comes up and walks by your side" while you are on the road to any Emmaus (Luke 24:15). It is the Christ Mystery that appears and grabs each of us now and then on our journey until we finally "make our home" there (John 15:4) and anoint (literally "christen") the stone of that place (Genesis 28:18) as a place to return to. This is surely the fullest meaning of the Sabbath rest.

Your True Self has already introduced itself to you, or you would have not kept reading this book. It would all be impossible fantasy talk. "It is not because you do not know the truth that I am writing to you, but rather because you know it already," John so beautifully puts it (1 John 2:21). You *do* know it.

John Duns Scotus (1265–1308), the Franciscan philosopher, whom I studied for four years, called each soul a unique "thisness" (*haecceity*), and he said it was to be found in every act of creation in its singularity. For him, God did not create universals, genus, and species, or anything that needed to come back again and again to get it right (reincarnation), but only specific and unique incarnations of the Eternal Mystery—each one chosen, loved, and preserved in existence as itself—*by being itself*. And this is the glory of God! As usual, Gerard Manley Hopkins, a poet deeply influenced by Scotus, says it best:

Each mortal thing does one thing and the same:
Deals out that being indoors each one dwells;
Selves—goes itself; myself it speaks and spells.
Crying: "What I do is me: for that I came."[11]

THE GREAT ALLOWER

In this regard, God is the Great Allower, despite all the attempts of ego, culture, and even religion to prevent God from allowing. Show me where God does not allow. God lets women be raped and raped women conceive, God lets tyrants succeed, and God lets me make my own mistakes again and again. He does not enforce his own commandments. God's total allowing of everything has in fact become humanity's major complaint. Conservatives so want God to smite sinners that they find every natural disaster to be a proof of just that, and then they invent some of their own smiting besides. Liberals reject God because God allows holocausts and torture and does not fit inside their seeming logic. If we were truly being honest, God is both a scandal and a supreme disappointment to most of us. We would prefer a God of domination and control to a God of allowing, as most official prayers make clear.

Both God and the True Self need only to fully be themselves and generously show themselves. Then the major work is done. The Source will always flow out, through, and toward those who want it. I would go so far as to define God as a "deep allowing" to the point of scandalous "cooperation with evil," both natural disasters and human evils. To allow yourself to be grabbed and held by such a divine wholeness is a dark and dangerous risk, and yet this is exactly what we mean by "salvation." We are allowing the Great Allower to allow us, even at our worst. We gradually learn to share in the divine freedom and must forgive God for being far too generous. This is not my "liberal" idea; Jesus says the same thing (see Matthew 20:15), but we cannot hear it for some reason.

Once your soul comes to its True Self, it can amazingly let go and be almost anything except selfish or separate. It can also not be anything that you need it to be or others want it to be. The soul is a natural at detachment and nonaddiction. It does not cling or grasp. It has already achieved its purpose in pure being more than in any specific doing of this or that. It can daringly and dangerously say with St. Paul, "For me there are no forbidden things, but not everything does good. For me there are no forbidden things, but I am not going to let anything dominate me either" (1 Corinthians 6:12). Finally we have become a human being instead of just a human doing. This is what we are practicing when we sit quietly in prayer: we are practicing under-doing and assured failure, which radically rearranges our inner hardware after a while. Soulful people, invariably humble and honest about themselves, are also risk takers: they both know the rules and how to break the rules properly. The True Self neither postures nor pretends. As Augustine said, the redeemed soul "loves God and does what it wills," which is not as simple as it sounds. It comes down to this: the soul and the True Self know that "my life is not about me, but I am about life."[12] The True Self is both very special and not special at all—in the very same moment. It has everything in general so it needs nothing in particular, as my father, St. Francis, might put it.

Most of humanity is so enchanted with its False (concocted) Self that it has largely doubted and rejected—or never known—its True Self. And so it lives in anxiety and insecurity. We have put so much time into creating it that we cannot imagine this False Self not being true—or not being "me." Even many believers spend much of their life manicuring and manufacturing a now very "Christian" False Self, while the core self or True Self is not touched or revealed at all (Ephesians 4:24). It is largely a game of ego pretend and in the end does not work. Only the False Self wants to be the most orthodox Catholic in Philadelphia, or the best Republican in Alabama, or needs to prove its heterosexuality. The True Self, with dear Mother Mary, knows only that "the Almighty has done great things for me, and Holy is his name" (Luke 1:48).

We have thus become a fragile and fragmented society, even though on so many other levels we are developed and civilized, each of us begging to be noticed and taken seriously by others, each hoping for our twenty minutes of fame. Ironically, we have not taken ourselves seriously or let God take us seriously if we still need to do this. Today most political and cultural fads change with the wind, today's political spin, manufactured headlines, and prime-time news that must fill up twenty-three minutes of "news." In a False Self world, there is nothing but fashion and display, and the amazing thing is that people bother to believe it or buy any of it. We are indeed slaves to Madison Avenue or "Mad Men." No wonder the Buddhists boldly call it all "emptiness."

This False Self world is sad and fragile. Yet the answer we seek is already inside each of us and largely resolved — not fashion but fact. Our True Self knows that there is no place to go or to get to. We are already at home — free and filled. That is the essence of the good news. What else would be "good news for *all* the people," which is what the angels promised the Bethlehem shepherds (Luke 2:10)? But it seems we would prefer a win-lose world, even if most lose. We are even willing to think of ourself as a loser or failure than dare to allow the Great Allower to do a win-win for what is perhaps God's only universe.

THE SPACIOUS SOUL

There is something in you that is not touched by coming and going, by up and down, by for or against, by the raucous teams of totally right or totally wrong. There is a part of you that is patient with both goodness and evil to gradually show themselves, exactly as God does. There is a part of you that does not rush to judgment. Rather, it stands vigilant and patient in the tragic gap that almost every moment offers. It is a riverbed of mercy. It is vast, silent, restful, and resourceful, and it receives and also lets go of all the comings and goings. It is *awareness itself* (as opposed to judgment itself), and awareness is not as such "thinking." It refuses to be pulled into the emotional and mental tugs of war that most of life is—before it is forever over and gone. To look out from this untouchable silence is what we mean by contemplation. In her *Interior Castle*, St. Teresa of Avila says, "The soul is spacious, plentiful, and its amplitude is impossible to exaggerate . . . the sun here radiates to every part . . . and nothing can diminish its beauty."[13] This is your soul. It is God-in-you. This is your True Self.

And you know what? Your soul is much larger than you! You are just along for the ride. When you learn to live there, you live with everyone and everything else too. Any language of exclusion or superiority no longer makes sense to you. Inside your True Self, you know you are not alone, and you foundationally "belong" to God and to the universe (1 Corinthians 3:23). You no longer have to work to feel important. You *are* intrinsically important, and it has all been "done unto you" (Luke 1:38), just as it was with Mary, who made no claims of worthiness *or* unworthiness. And if God so gratuitously and graciously includes you here and now in this world, why would such a God change God's mind in the next world? Love is the one eternal thing and takes away your foundational fear of death. This is very good stuff.

As Isaiah so poetically said to Israel, "Where is your mother's writ of divorce? To which of my creditors have I sold you? ... Has my hand become too short to save?" (50:1–2). Or did Jesus change his regular policy after his resurrection, and his love become exclusionary and conditional, as it never was during his lifetime? In fact, his breath, perfect Shalom, and divine forgiveness have all become the very same thing after the Resurrection (John 20:22) and given freely to the crowd who had just totally let him down and are hiding behind locked doors. The community of saints *is* the community of sinners.

You do not create your True Self, or earn it, or work up to it by any moral or ritual behavior whatsoever. It is all and forever mercy for all of us and all the time, and there are no exceptions. You do not climb up to your True Self. You fall into it, so don't avoid all falling. There, ironically and happily, you are finally found. And you notice your small False Self almost as a disappointing afterthought. All people have access to their True Self from their very first inhalation and exhalation, which we now know is the very sound of the sacred name Yahweh. We breathe God in and out—much more than we "know" God, understand God, or even talk to God.[14]

God has not been wasting our time here, and God will not be found ineffective, failing, or unfaithful toward what Divinity has created. "We may be unfaithful, but God is always faithful, for he cannot disown *his own self*" (2 Timothy 2:13).

Dionysius the Areopagite, a sixth-century mystical theologian, said that we start the spiritual path thinking we are pulling on a chain that is attached to heaven. Only midway in the journey do we realize that the chain we thought we were pulling is instead pulling us — toward an alluring brilliance.[15] We each set out trying to create our own hand-cut and hand-made diamond; but experienced pilgrims tell us that the diamond was first made by Another, and it is indeed drawing us forward into a brilliance that is now uniquely *ours*.

CHAPTER 2

What Is "The False Self"?

I cannot lose anything in this place of abundance I have found.
—ST. CATHERINE OF SIENA

I begin this chapter with a positive quote, so I can describe the False Self properly and avoid the usual connotations of *false*. Your False Self is not your bad self, your clever or inherently deceitful self, the self that God does not like or you should not like. Actually your False Self is quite good and necessary as far as it goes. It just does not go far enough, and it often poses and thus substitutes for the real thing. That is its only problem, and that is why we call it "false." The False Self is bogus more than bad, and bogus only when it pretends to be more than it is. Various false selves (temporary costumes) are necessary to get us all started, and they show their limitations when they stay around too long. If a person keeps growing, his or her various false selves usually die in exposure to greater light.

Your False Self, which we might also call your "small self," is your launching pad: your body image, your job, your education, your clothes, your money, your car, your sexual identity, your success, and so on. These are the trappings of ego that we all use to get us through an ordinary day. They are a nice enough platform to stand on, but they are largely a projection of our self-image and our attachment to it. When you are able to move beyond your False Self—at the right time and in the right way—*it will feel precisely as if you have lost nothing*. In fact, it will feel like freedom and liberation. When you are connected to the Whole, you no longer need to protect or defend the mere part. You are now connected to something inexhaustible.

To *not* let go of our False Self at the right time and in the right way is precisely what it means to be stuck, trapped, and addicted to yourself. (The traditional word for that was *sin*.) And it's not just a matter of chronological age. Some spiritually precocious children, usually those with a disability of some type, see through the False Self rather early. Some old men and old women are still dressing it up at my age (I'm sixty-nine now). If all you have at the end of your life is your False Self, there will not be much to eternalize. It is transitory. These costumes are all "accidents" largely created by the mental ego. Your False Self is what changes, passes, and dies when you die. Only your True Self lives forever.

There are *four major splits* from reality that we have all made in varying degrees to create our False Self:

1. We split from our shadow self and pretend to be our idealized self.
2. We split our mind from our body and soul and live in our minds.
3. We split life from death and try to live our life without any "death."
4. We split ourselves from other selves and try to live apart, superior, and separate.

Each of these four illusions must—and will—be overcome, either in this world, in our last days and hours, or afterward. (That is what Catholics meant by "purgatory." They gave us one final chance to get it!) Each of these splits from reality makes any experience of God or our True Self largely impossible. Spirituality, pure and simple, is overcoming these four splits and is the message of the rest of this book.

DISCOVERING THE FALSE SELF: THERAPY VERSUS SPIRITUAL DIRECTION

Who is telling us about the False Self today? Who is even equipped to tell us? Many clergy have not figured this out for themselves, since even ministry can be a career decision or an attraction to "religion" more than the result of an encounter with God or themselves. Formal religious status can maintain the False Self rather effectively, especially if there are a lot of social payoffs like special respect, titles, salaries, a "good" self-image, or nice costumes. It is no accident that the religious "Pharisees" become the symbolic bad guys in the Jesus story. Most Western therapies do not know about the True Self either, only about the many disguises of the False Self, which is what psychology should indeed be about. Even a good therapist often offers you good coping mechanisms for your particular False Self. It can recommend, perhaps, that you be more sociable at the superficial cocktail party so you can make friends. An immature therapy might encourage women to be codependent and adjust to an unhealthy husband for the sake of the children. It really has no choice but to teach you how to survive and fit in the world as it is. My dear friend Dr. Gerald May used to say that his own field of psychiatry often helped people "cope" or "meddle," and little more. In fact, some counseling helps you adjust to an often sick and immature world or church and must call that "health." *There is a comfortable contract between personal egos and an entire egoic culture.* We don't tell on one another, and we both find it quite agreeable to let one another off the hook of truth. Mutual and false flattery is the name of the game (1 John 2:15–17) in most systems. We too often prefer accolades to actual achievement.

Good therapy often gives you survival strategies around other False Selves, which is most of the public world of commerce, politics, entertainment, and big league athletics. I am not being negative or unkind in saying that. Therapy has to work within the world as it is, so what else can it do? It has no knowledge of the whole, the permanent, the sacred, or the really real. It cannot even speak of the "higher power" as AA does. Psychology of itself has no access beyond the False Self, its illusions and inherent fragility (except for some types of transpersonal or archetypal psychology), so it just tries to make it work—and for now. Master teachers like the Buddha see the False Self courageously; they forthrightly call it "emptiness" and the True Self "enlightenment." Knowledge of your True Self gradually places your life in a big and ever bigger frame. Then the small stuff can no longer hurt you or define you for the long term.

Therapy is not equipped to call the small stuff into question—things like ever higher pay, more vacation days, not being noticed, taking offense. That is the job of religion, the ultimate clearinghouse, and why spiritual direction is a different discipline than therapeutic counseling is. You can do both, as I do. Good spiritual direction will highly simplify and clarify your therapy, and good therapy will ground any spiritual direction in honesty and necessary shadow boxing. Good therapy will allow you to cope with greater serenity and efficiency because you will learn how to do your human job well and with personal satisfaction. True spiritual direction can link that human job with your divine job without dismissing the human job in the least.

Hospice workers who have accompanied many deaths can tell you about this much better than I can. They often start as de facto therapists and cannot help but end up as spiritual directors by simply observing the process of transformation from False Self to True Self in the dying process. Kathleen Dowling Singh goes so far as to say that "*the life and death of a human being is exquisitely calibrated to automatically produce union with Spirit*" at the end.[1]

Therapists deal largely with the psychological self, because the profession as such cannot address the ontological, metaphysical, theological self. That is a very different level of being. A good counselor helps us with our relative identity as son or daughter, parent, spouse, gay person, employee, and so on, because there is no agreed-on way to talk about our absolute identity in professional therapeutic circles. They cannot risk "God language" because it has been cheapened by centuries of less-than-helpful use. Many religious people use God talk far too glibly, too quickly, and naively, and each religious denomination has its own vocabulary, land mines, and agreed-on clichés. Thus, the professional world of psychology naturally mistrusts religion and backs away from any reference to the transcendent or the "transpersonal self" or even a Higher Power. Any kind of God talk is still risky and embarrassing for many counseling departments, and they are rightly afraid of it. But I do not have to be. I often think I have the greatest job in the world as I try to put it all together.

In a way, much of therapy is only delaying the essential problem of ego and the meaning of existence until the deathbed. As Stephen Levine said in his classic study *Who Dies?*, "If you made a list of everything you own, everything you think of as you, everything that you prefer, that list would be the distance between you and the living truth."[2] For me, "the living truth" *is* the True Self. It is also why James Hillman, the brilliant Jungian psychologist, sincerely wrote, "We've had a hundred years of therapy—and the world's getting worse," in his book of the same name.[3] If that is sadly true, it is just an honest statement about the inherent limitations of any system except the biggest.

Healthy religion should be the most inclusive system of all, making use of every discipline, avenue, and access point for Big Truth. Personal therapy, based in paid counseling sessions, as brilliant as it is, still often creates co-dependencies, its own in-house problems for which it has its own in-house answers, and just like the clergy and scientific medicine, it needs to say, "Come back again next week!" These professions are not as free as spiritual teachers or alternative medicines to say, "That is a false problem to begin with," or, "You are living in the wrong frame of life," or, "Once you get it, you don't need me anymore."

Jesus did not "cure" people of their mere medical or physical ailment; he actually "healed" them and sent them on their way or back to society. In other words, he gave them not just new software, but a new "motherboard." Jesus, and all other true spiritual teachers, did not just offer people helpful life changes; they actually *changed them*. True healing says what Jesus said to the paralyzed man: To show you that you are also forgiven and forgiveness is what you really want and need, "Get up, pick up your mat, and go home!" Act on a truth, and only then does it become *your* truth. (Matthew 9:6). The real healing for the paralyzed man was the courage to act *as if* — and then his mind and body followed in step.

This total realignment of the self is often portrayed in the Gospels as new self-confidence, new capacities for relationship, new joy, forgiveness of the old self — and all of these are made recognizable by the physical cure. (I am not denying physical healing; in fact, I have seen it happen more than once, even in myself.). The Bible did not have all the abstract psychospiritual, cultural, and relational language we have today. The biblical just saw embodied people not making it in life — and then making it again. They knew something had indeed happened in another person's mind and soul, and not just his or her body. We now know they were right about what we call psychosomatic diseases. Bodies, minds, and souls do operate as one.

CONTINUING THE WALKABOUT

Your False Self is who you think you are. Your thinking does not make it true. Your False Self is almost entirely a social construct to get you started on your life journey. It is a set of agreements between your childhood and your parents, your family, your neighbors, your school chums, your partner or spouse, and your religion. It is your "container" for your separate self.[4] Jesus would call it your "wineskin," which he points out usually cannot hold any new wine (Mark 2:21–22). Your ego container likes to stay "contained" and hates change.

Your False Self is how you define yourself outside of love, relationship, or divine union. After you have spent many years laboriously building this separate self, with all its labels and preoccupations, you are very attached to it. And why wouldn't you be? It's what you know and all you know. To move beyond it will always feel like losing or dying. Perhaps you have noticed that master teachers like Jesus and the Buddha, St. Francis, all the "Teresas" (Avila, Lisieux, and Calcutta), Hafiz, Kabir, and Rumi talk about dying much more than we are comfortable with. They all know that if you do not learn the art of dying and letting go early, you will hold onto your False Self far too long, until it kills you anyway.

A recent TV show on the Amish revealed a broad disbelief that anybody could so wholeheartedly forgive the man who murdered their children in 2006, as the Amish appeared to do. Then the commentator recognized that the Amish are totally practiced in letting go and dying to self. They know they are connected to and part of a much larger divine reality, which looks naive to the rest of us. But letting go of life, hurts, and grudges is much more possible for them than for most of the rest of us. These "plain folks" might have a limited and limiting worldview on other counts by some standards, but on the foundations as to what is real and what is passing, they are experts and lead the way. It probably explains their peace and their seeming happiness and contentment, which surely is not true for most of us.

I would say the same of Mother Teresa's sisters, whom I lived with for several weeks at the motherhouse in Calcutta shortly after she died. Both the Amish and the Missionaries of Charity so concentrate on the True Self in God that they almost disdain the False Self. They offer a shining witness of radical living in the True Self in a largely False Self world. That is what monks, friars, and nuns were supposed to symbolize in a culture. You are doing the same thing every time you sit in silence, refusing to produce and perform. We call it a "contemplative sit," and do it at least once a day until the False Self shows itself as ephemeral and passing and we are realigned in truth.

It was Thomas Merton, the Cistercian monk, who first suggested the use of the term *False Self*. He did this to clarify for many Christians the meaning of Jesus' central and oft-repeated teaching that we must die to ourselves, or "lose ourselves to find ourselves" (Mark 8:35). This quote has caused much havoc and pushback in Christian history because it sounds negative and ascetical, and it was usually interpreted as an appeal to punish the body. But its intent is personal liberation, not self-punishment. Centuries of Christians falsely assumed that if they could "die" to their body, their spirit would for some reason miraculously arise.

Apart from a general Platonic denial of the body in most religions, Paul made a most unfortunate choice of the word *flesh* as the very enemy of *Spirit* (for example, Galatians 5:16–24). Now we would probably say "ego" or "small self," which would be much closer to his actual intended meaning. Remember that Christianity is the religion that believes "the Word became flesh" (John 1:13), and Jesus even returned to the "flesh" after the Resurrection (Luke 24:40) — so flesh cannot be bad for us. If it is in any way antibody, it is never authentic Christianity. Merton rightly recognized that it was not the body that had to "die" but the "false self" that we do not need anyway. It becomes a too-easy substitute for our deeper and deepest truth.

DIVERSIONARY TACTICS

Much of the Christian religion, in misunderstanding and seeking to avoid the major death of the False Self, became moralistic instead, piously and falsely "sacrificial" about many arbitrary and small things. I guess we thought this pleased Jesus — who actually saw through it all and denied any idealization of sacrifice or false generosity and the payback that it always expects. In another book I called it "the myth of sacrifice."[5] "Sacrifice" usually leads to a well-hidden sense of entitlement and perpetuates the vicious circle of merit, a mind-set that leads most of us to assume that we are more deserving than others because of what we have given or done. As the old saying goes, all expectations and self-sacrifice are just resentments waiting to happen. Jesus came to end all false sacrificial notions, I believe, and he did it once and for all (Hebrews 7:27, 10:10–15).

But the ego and egoic culture led us right back into it, probably because the False Self rightly feels so unworthy that it must earn a sense of worthiness through some notion of heroism or hard work. Even rich white men who are born into their money will somehow let you know how much they "sacrificed" to get what they have. When you sacrifice, you always "deserve." Sacrifice, much more than we care to admit, creates entitlement, a "you-owe-me" attitude, and a well-hidden sense of superiority.

Jesus brilliantly said, "Go, learn the meaning of the words, 'What I want is mercy and not sacrifice.'" It seems to have been one of his favorite lines from Hosea (Matthew 9:13, 12:7), although it was a risky and dangerous idea in a religion still based in temple tithes and the sacrifice of animals and grains. Jesus knew that most notions of sacrifice largely appeal to our False Self, are not needed by the True Self, and are almost always manipulated and misused by people, most institutions, and warring nations. Just ask any member of Al-Anon where "sacrifice" got them and their family. It is now called "enabling" behavior — where the supposed sacrifice enables the addict's destructive behavior; it doesn't help at all.

I agree with French anthropologist and philosopher René Girard when he says that Jesus came to end sacrificial religion itself. Sacrifice and asceticism are usually indicators of False Self religion, as the Buddha himself eventually discovered. Jesus was criticized because he was not ascetic like John the Baptist (Mark 2:18), and it is amazing that this has been part of our selective forgetfulness. Ascetic practices have far too much social and ego payoff, which is why Jesus advised against anything pious or generous being done publicly (Matthew 6:1–4, 16–18): "Don't even let your left hand know what your right hand is doing," he says. External religion is also dangerous religion.

Jesus, along with Buddha, had a much more foundational death to walk us through than mere personal heroics or public grandstanding. They point to an eventual and essential "renouncing" of the False Self, which will always be the essential death. It is at the heart of the spiritual journey. Ken Wilber often describes it dramatically and without apology.[6] Many of us have learned in contemplative practice that it all starts with dying to our own addictive, compulsive, and negative ways of processing reality. That is the biggest and hardest death of all, and it has no social payoff or immediate satisfaction whatsoever. There is no full recovery from addiction, Bill Wilson said, until we have achieved actual "emotional sobriety."[7] *Contemplation is the ultimate recovery, because it is from the universal addiction to our own preferred way of thinking.* This is much harder than any single moral battle with any single moral issue.

The distinction must not be between body and soul or spirit, but between falsity and truth. The body holds much truth, and the soul, mind, and heart can hold onto some very dangerous lies, including arrogance, ambition, pride, conceit, vanity, hatred, and prejudice. The only important question is always, "Is it true?" not, "Is it in the body or in the spirit?" I live in a church that rewards people at the highest levels for obvious sins of the "spirit" and punishes people at the communion table for possible mistakes of the flesh. Jesus was almost exactly the opposite because he knew that sins of the flesh are usually not sins of malice but of weakness, whereas sins of the spirit proceed from a cold heart, a superior and separate False Self, and thus a denied soul. "Circumcise your heart and not your flesh" is the insightful and honest Jewish teaching (Deuteronomy 10:16; Jeremiah 9:26) from a religion that mandated physical male circumcision as much as Christians mandate baptism. I remember my novice master warning us in 1961 that too many priests and other religious were "pure as angels but proud as devils."

THE PROCCUPATIONS OF THE FALSE SELF

It is sadly true that most institutions and nations admire and reward sins of the "spirit," and various forms of arrogance and greed often lead to promotions and praise. But pride, ambition, and vanity are still pride, ambition, and vanity; they do not stop being capital sins because someone is pope or president. "Greed is good" in America, extravagant bonuses are envied and imitated, and careerism is rampant among the clergy. (This is not just my judgment but a statement of the Vatican Office for Bishops a few years ago.) Sins of the flesh, however, carry shame and guilt and can always be used to bring anybody down in church, culture, or the state.

This is the precise denotation of the phrase "the world" in the New Testament (1 John 2:15–17). The word *world* as it is usually used in the New Testament is a way of speaking of the corporate False Self. "World" is not speaking of creation, the planet, or nature, but what we might call "the system." This confusion has created many Christians totally enamored with the "dirty rotten system," as Dorothy Day called it, while showing no concern for earth care, animals, or global warming—whoever caused it. What a strange and sad turnaround from the original intention

"The world" in the Bible is the system of mutual flattery and constant rewarding of the False Self. Jesus said, "In the world [system] you will have trouble; but be brave, I have already overcome it" (John 16:33). He overcame the system's seduction and illusion by living inside an utterly different frame of reference, the eternal "Reign of God." The False Self is no longer a threat or an enduring attraction once you see the True Self. This is what we are trying to say when Christians sing in a dozen ways at Easter, "Jesus destroyed death!" Probably people would understand this much better if we said, "Jesus exposed the lie," because there is clearly plenty of death moving around that has not died. But once the veil is pulled back from illusion, it is just a matter of time. God's time is patient time.

Our False Self does not let go easily. But that doesn't mean the False Self should be attacked or eliminated. In time, it will reveal itself for the false wizard that it is. If you go out after it directly, it will only disguise itself further, while you in the meantime get to feel quite virtuous. It is like giving up candy for Lent. It might affect your willpower, self-image, or waistline (which might be good), but your soul will be largely untouched. Too many true believers have attacked the devil in a quite devilish way. But the world is tired of hateful religion, as it well should be.

What the ego (the False Self) hates and fears more than anything else is change. It will think up a thousand other things to be concerned about or be moralistic about — anything rather than giving up "who I think I am" and "who I need to be to look good." Seeking any kind of higher moral ground, as we are almost all trained to do, is often a way of avoiding the death of the False Self, which is why Jesus so often mistrusts moral achievement contests. The False Self will create minor moral victories (like people who are scrupulous about church attendance or doctrinal minutiae) to avoid the major and necessary ones (like underpaying their employees or demeaning their wife). As Jesus put it, "You will strain out gnats and swallow camels" (Matthew 23:24).

The ego, and also the corporate ego, is often personified in world Scriptures as the devil or Satan. How else do you give "reality" to something like evil that must be taken seriously? You personify it. The devil's secret is always disguised, as we see with the snake in Genesis, where he is called "the most subtle of all the wild beasts that God had made" (3:1). Satan does not tempt you so much to the "hot sins" like greed, lust, and gross ambition. They are too obviously evil and will eventually show themselves as such. Instead Satan tempts you to do proper, defensible, and often admired things, but for cold, malicious, or self-centered reasons. Maybe we cannot see this pattern because *we actually admire the glamour of evil* (1 John 2:15–17), *and we often disdain the seeming weakness of holiness and virtue* (2 Corinthians 12:9–10). Nuns who work in the inner city are not taken too seriously, while we envy city bosses who are being driven in stretch limousines. We do. We really do!

As C. S. Lewis said, the devil will not appear with a pitchfork and horns, but will show up dressed in a three-piece suit. Changing our drinking habits and addiction to pornography makes us feel stronger and more moral—and it should. But changing our career status, compassion for the "little people," or lowering our prices makes us feel slow, naive, and foolish—and it shouldn't. Goodness and evil are both well disguised as long as you live in your False Self. That is the core of the problem and why Jesus is about a foundational change of the self rather than any cosmetic "moral changes." The first is mystical spirituality; the second is moralistic religion, which is most of what we know. God surely knows that most people are not malicious as much as mistaken, not deceitful as much as deceived, not ill willed but just terribly ignorant of their True Selves.

You see now why faith is the "narrow way that few follow upon" (Matthew 7:14). The True Self never knows with absolutely surety that it is right or "good," but in fact it does not even need to, which is what we mean by "faith." The True Self has knocked on both the hard bottom and the high ceiling of reality and has less and less need for mere verbal certitudes or answers that always fit. It has found its certainty elsewhere and now lives inside a YES that is so big that it can absorb most of the little noes. The False Self fears and denies all seeming contradictions, probably because it unconsciously knows that it is itself a mass of contradictions and is searching for some external order or control. You can forgive the outer world only if and when you have first forgiven your own inner world.

The True Self has already overcome the contradictions and paradoxes of life, which is symbolized by the Risen Christ who presents the full tension of death and life, earth and spirit, human and divine — and *precisely as overcome*. That is the standing message that the Resurrected One holds for all of history. He *holds and overcomes the ultimate and major tensions of humanity*.

In one glorious body, he unites our highest aspirations with the very deepest flesh of our being — which heals everything. Breath and clay are again one, and Adam has been re-created. Have you ever wondered why Christian art invariably shows the Risen Christ carrying a big banner, but there is seldom anything written on it? Maybe we do not know the message yet. Well, here it is! "*Love is stronger than death*" is the message of Easter.

THE MYTH OF SEPARATENESS

All mature religion must and will talk about the death of any notion of a separate, and therefore False Self, while recognizing that only a deep security in a larger love will give you the courage to do that. The True Self can let go because it is radically safe at its core. The True Self is like a baby crawling away from its mother (God). The baby knows she will grab him back if there is any danger whatsoever. What confidence and security that gives the True Self. The separate self *is* the False Self, and the False Self thus needs to overdefine itself as unique, special, superior, and adequate. What a trap. So Jesus must say, "Unless the *single* grain of wheat dies, it remains just a *single* grain" (John 12:24). "But if it does die, it will bear much fruit!"

Whenever you are loving someone or something else, you have died on some level—and let go of your separate self. As Stephen Levine said so often, our fear of death largely comes from "the imagined loss of an imagined individuality."[8] Neither of these seeming losses is a loss at all but actually an expansion. Please think and pray about that. It will allow you to overcome your fear of death. Our False Self is precisely our individual singularity in both its "Aren't I wonderful!" or "Aren't I terrible!" forms. Both are their own kind of ego trip, and both take the tiny little self far too seriously. The true saint is no longer surprised at his littleness or her greatness. A mouse in a mansion does not need to take lessons in humility. Both your goodness and your badness are always common domain. Any notion of a private and personal heaven is by definition not a heaven you can "go" to. In fact, it is precisely and exactly hell. If you are hoping for your well-earned crown, harp, and white robe, it is your False Self that is doing the hoping.

This is why Jesus mocks the silly religious arguments about who is married to whom in heaven. And he says, in effect, that you have missed the whole point (Luke 20:27–40). We are all to be "children of the resurrection" (20:36) in a new kind of "aliveness" (20:38) which is based not on singularity but precisely on *communion*. Only the True Self understands and enjoys that, whereas the False Self feels diminished.

"Firstness" is a need for only the fragile False Self. "Lastness" has no real meaning or significance for the True Self or the soul. How can you be last when you belong to the whole body? "If the ear were to say, 'I am not an eye and therefore I am not a part of the Body,' would that mean it was not a part of the Body? In fact, it is the so-called weakest parts of the Body that are the most indispensable ones (1 Corinthians 12:15–22). The True Self sees everything in wholes and therefore in contrast to the way the world sees things, which now appears upside down to them. The

False Self sees everything in parts and hierarchies and in reference to itself, which is not to see very well at all.

Before transformation, sin is any kind of moral mistake; afterward, *sin is a mistake about who you are and whose you are.* In that sense, only the False Self can and will sin. The False Self tells lies because it somehow *is* a lie. It steals because it has allowed itself to be stolen. As Jesus said to those who were killing him, false selves "do not even know what they are doing" (Luke 23:34). The True Self is conscious, the False Self is largely unconscious, and you do evil only when you are unconscious.

In short, the False Self is a house built on sand (Matthew 7:26). Fortunately God is willing to work with sand, and created sand too. The sands of life are still the tunnel through which we dig to get to the immortal diamond. You can and will still make mistakes when your home base is the True Self, but you will now see them for what they are — mistakes — and be able to apologize and change.

It is very important that you know that *the True Self is not moral perfection or even psychological wholeness.* Many masochistic saints, eccentric prophets, and neurotic mystics are more than a bit strange, and they almost always have serious blind spots, but *they knew who they were in God and they knew how to return there.* That is their secret. The True Self can see and speak truth to itself and also recognize its own games, if not immediately then eventually. It is a house, therefore, built on rock (Matthew 7:25), which does not mean it does not need constant maintenance, cleaning, and refinishing. The True Self is not the perfect self. It merely participates in the One who is. *Holiness is not always wholeness; in fact, it never is.* God alone is whole and "good," as Jesus says—when even he is called "good" (Mark 10:18). I hope that frees you to be less judgmental of others and more patient with yourself too.

A PARABLE

When you get your "I am" right, morality tends to finally take care of itself. If you still have your "I am" wrong, especially toward the end of your life, even your virtues will become a burden for others. You can see this in Jesus' immense impatience with the Pharisees and teachers of the law, who are always trying to trap him and trip him up in his words—all in the name of orthodoxy.

As always the literati say it best, in this case the marvelous short story from author Flannery O'Connor, in her masterpiece "Revelation." In that story, her main character, Ruby Turpin, a good but righteous Christian, has a vision as she stands in a pigpen. Ruby is a classic Christian False Self, who finally looks out and beyond her self-made holiness (her "pigpen") to her first glimpses of her True Self. In the story, she describes what she sees as a "vast horde of souls" rumbling toward heaven: poor whites, black people in white robes, and "battalions of freaks and lunatics shouting and clapping and leaping like frogs." Bringing up the rear, she says, is a "tribe of people like her," who "had always had a little of everything" and were marching "behind the others with great dignity, accountable as they always had been for good order and common sense and respectable behavior.... Yet she could see by their shocked and altered faces that even their virtues were being burned away."[9] There it is, as only a master teacher can teach it. O'Connor presents the False Self in its final shattering moments. One only hopes that Ruby can surrender and begin to sing "off-key" like the rumbling hordes. She has suffered from a massive case of mistaken identity all of her life, just as we all do, but hers was bolstered by a strong "Christian" False Self. Religion can significantly delay the emergence of our True Self. I have been a priest for forty-two years and can say that from solid experience.

The True Self does not really "go to heaven" as much as live there already. It is indeed part of a "vast horde rumbling toward heaven." It lives in the big Body now, puts little trust in its private virtue, and feels no undue surprise at its personal weakness. Ruby is just opening up to heaven for the first time, and she is a little shocked and surely disappointed that so many "others" are there.

The True Self includes everybody who wants to join in. It is almost too simple and straightforward, this "vast horde rumbling toward heaven." Some call it "the communion of saints." Some thought of it as the church. Already in the fourth century, St. Augustine said something quite shocking but surely true: "The church is precisely the state of communion of the whole world" (*Ecclesiam in totius orbis communione consistere*). Thomas Aquinas, no lightweight for Catholic ears, said things that few Catholics or clergy would even agree with today. He spoke of the church "existing since Abel" (Hebrews 11:4) and that "the body of the church is constituted by the people who existed from the beginning of the world until now."[10] Wherever there is faith, hope, and charity, there is the church and there is God, and that is the primary church I believe in.

In ordinary language, the True Self is held together by the glue of a universal love. "For God is love and anyone who lives in love lives in God, and God lives in him" (1 John 4:16). When we live in such abundance, we do not need to fight or defeat our False Self. It naturally fades into the background in the presence of absolute abundance and absolute allowing.

The beautiful body and life that Jesus surrendered on the cross were willingly surrendered not because they were bad or unworthy, but because they were *no longer necessary or helpful to the final task*. The hard mining operation of sifting through the slag and refuse that once appeared so important is eventually done. It was once important but it no longer is. "There is a time for everything" as Ecclesiastes so wisely says (3:1ff.).

We do not really find the immortal diamond of the True Self. It gradually appears as we do the work of growing up, just as the Risen One randomly appeared as a friend on the road, was confused with the gardener, showed up in a locked room, and came for breakfast on the beach. Let the master, Thomas Merton, say it, as he so often does: "A door opens in the center of our being, and we seem to fall through it into immense depths, which although they are infinite — are still accessible to us. All eternity seems to have become ours in this one placid and breathless contact."[11]

This door needs to open only once in your lifetime, and you will forever know where home base is. You will henceforth be dissatisfied with anything less. First, second, and third base got you there, but you would not think of running back to them.

THE SONG OF TRUE SELF

Within us there is an inner, natural dignity. (You often see it in older folks.)

An inherent worthiness that already knows and enjoys. (You see it in children.)

It is an immortal diamond waiting to be mined and is never discovered undesired.

It is a reverence humming within you that must be honored.

Call it the soul, the unconscious, deep consciousness, or the indwelling Holy Spirit.

Call it nothing.

It does not need the right name or right religion to show itself.

It does not even need to be understood. It is usually wordless.

It just is, and shows itself best when we are silent, or in love, or both.

I will call it the True Self here.

It is God-in-All-Things yet not circumscribed by any one thing.

It is enjoyed only when each part is in union with all other parts, because only then does it stand in the full truth.

Once in a while, this True Self becomes radiant and highly visible in one lovely place or person.

Superbly so, and for all to see, in the body of the Risen Christ.

And note that I did say "body." It begins here and now in our embodied state in this world. Thus, the Christ Mystery travels the roads of time.

Once you have encountered this True Self—and once is more than enough—the False Self will begin to fall away on its own.

This will take most of your life, however, just as it did in Jesus.

CHAPTER 3

What Dies and Who Lives?

 At heart, one does not feel that he is going to die, he only feels sorry for the man next to him.

ERNEST BECKER, THE DENIAL OF DEATH

"My God is not a god of the dead, but of the living! For to him, all people are in fact, alive!" Jesus said to "those who did not believe in resurrection."

LUKE 20:38 AND 27

In one way or another, almost all religions say that you must die before you die, and then you will know what dying means—and what it does not mean! Your usual viewing platform is utterly inadequate to see what is real. It is largely useless to talk about the very ground of your being, your True Self, or your deepest soul until you have made real contact with these at least once. That demands dying to the old viewing platform of the mental ego and the

False Self. There is just no way around that. If you do make contact, you forever know that something is there that can be talked about, relied on, and deeply trusted. You move from religion as mere belief to religion as a new kind of knowing.

Henceforth, you know you have a soul, and your soul becomes your primary receiver station from then on. Most souls are initially "unsaved" in the sense that they cannot dare to imagine they could be one with God/Reality/the universe. This is the lie of the False Self that dies slowly, and only after much testing from our side. Many clergy fight me on the idea of actual oneness with God the most. It is as if they do not believe in their own product. No wonder so few are buying into their half-hearted message.

Only your soul can know the soul of other things. Only a part can recognize the whole from which it came. But first something within you, your True Self, must be awakened. Those who have not made contact with their own souls will think you are talking gibberish and silliness when you talk about spiritual things (1 Corinthians 2:10–16), and they are just being honest with their limited experience. Conversely, many religious people will defend their own lack of any God experience by calling you a "heretic" or wrong, because you are speaking beyond their limited experience. They are sincere, too, although often not very humble or very kind (I get my cruelest letters from religious people). This is exactly why Jesus said, "All will hate you because of me" (Luke 21:17), and even, "Blessed are you when they hate you" (Luke 6:22). He wanted us to be prepared for this common surprise.

There is indeed such a thing as heresy, and I am trained and believe in such a thing as orthodoxy (although the word is not found in the Scriptures), yet Jesus' entire life drama makes it clear that the biggest heretics are very often running the show. Is it possible to read the accounts of hostility, persecution, passion, and the murder of Jesus in any other way? The religious False Self is the best and the most defended self of all. When God has become our personal and group lackey, we can hate, oppress, torture, and kill others with total impunity. The religious False Self can even justify racism, slavery, war, and total denial or deception and feel no guilt whatsoever, because "they think they are doing a holy duty for God" (John 16:2). The ego has found its cover, so be quite careful about being religious. If your religion does not transform your consciousness to one of compassion, it is more a part of the problem than any solution.

The reason we must die before we die is expressed eloquently by Kathleen Dowling Singh, a woman who has spent her life in hospice work: *"The ordinary mind [the False Self] and its delusions die in the 'Nearing Death Experience.' As death carries us off, it is impossible to any longer pretend that who we are is our ego. The ego is transformed in the very carrying off."*[1] Some form of death—psychological, spiritual, relational, or physical—is the only way we will loosen our ties to our small and separate False Self. Only then does it return in a new shape, which I am calling the Risen Christ, or the soul, or the True Self.

The ego self is the self before death; the soul is real only after we have walked through the death of our ever fading False Self and come out larger and brighter on the other side. Hafiz, the fourteenth-century Persian mystic poet, says it as only he can: "God is trying to sell you something, but you don't want to buy. This is what your suffering is: Your fantastic haggling, your manic screaming over the price!"[2]

Anything less than the death of the False Self is useless religion. The False Self must die for the True Self to live or, as Jesus himself puts it, "Unless I go, the Spirit cannot come" (John 16:7). This is rather clear but also devastating news. Theologically speaking, let me put it this way: Jesus (a good person) still had to die for the Christ (the universal presence) to arise. It is the pattern of transformation, but the letting go of the original "good person" is always a huge leap of faith precisely because it is deemed to be so "good." Biblically it is foreshadowed in the killing of the innocent Passover lamb, which had been taken into the home and likely already named by the children (Exodus 12:5–6). What has to die is not usually bad; in fact, it will often feel good and necessary.

Your True Self is that part of you that is going to live forever and sees truthfully. It is divine breath passing through you. Your False Self is that part of you that is constantly changing and will eventually die anyway. It is in the world of passing *forms* and looks out with itself as the central reference point—which is never true. The False Self is passing, tentative, and, as the Hindus and Buddhists say, "empty." Mature religion helps us speed up this process of dying to the False Self—or at least to stop fighting its clear demise. This is why saints live in such a counter-cultural way. It is a free fall anyway, so we might as well jump in and cooperate, they seem to say. It is much easier to offer a free yes ahead of time before it is forced on us on our deathbed or in tragedy. St. Francis says in his lifetime, "Welcome, Sister Death!"

Your False Self is not bad or wrong; it is just mortal. It is relative and not absolute. It is passing and not substantial, a largely mental and cultural construct. It will die when you die. For some reason, it is easier for us to fall in love with that which dies and is dying than that which lives and lives forever. Maybe our love of our False Self is a kind of sympathy for what is fragile and needy, an understandable attachment to transitory things before they depart—knowing at least unconsciously that they will. That is not bad and in fact gets the whole ball rolling. *We grow big inside constricted space and situations*, although none of us wants to admit it. Some have said we would never grow up if we knew we were going to live forever in this world. I suspect that is true.

Your False Self is your necessary warm-up act, the ego part of you that establishes your separate identity, especially in the first half of life. Basically it is your incomplete self trying to pass for your whole self. We fall in love with the part so much that we deny the Whole. God surely understands that and is undoubtedly glad that we are at least in love with something. Such love gets us started until we eventually realize that "love lasts forever" (1 Corinthians 13:13) and is the one thing we can forever count on and forever *are*.

But do know this: *every time you choose to love, you have also just chosen to die.* Every time you truly love, you are letting go of yourself as an autonomous unit and have given a bit of yourself away to something or someone else, and it is not easily retrieved — unless you choose to stop loving — which many do. These first moments of ecstatic release from imprisonment in yourself are wonderful, erotic, and immensely life giving. Eventually, however, when that expanded self wants to retreat back into itself, it realizes it is trapped in a much larger truth now. It has a decision to make: it either expands — dying to its former small self — or enfolds back into itself, which is just another and worse kind of dying. But in either case, you die. T. S. Eliot says it more dramatically in the "Four Quartets":

The only hope, or else despair,
Lies in the choice of pyre or pyre —
To be redeemed from fire by fire.[3]

The realignment of our selves from two to One through a loving and lifelong tug of war is the very dance of transformation. It is a trust walk, a constant testing of the reliability of love and God (which you eventually know are the same), which eventually allows us to fall trustingly back into our True Self. Then we are one again.

Just remember, we are testing God much more than God is ever directly testing us. Your ordinary dualistic, either-or mind, your self-preservative ego, will refuse and avoid this "staggering change of perspective" by every means possible, so let's state it outlined and clearly:

What dies? Your False Self — and it is just a matter of WHEN, not IF.

Who lives? The God Self that has always lived, but now includes YOU.

And note that it is a WHAT that dies, and a WHO that lives!

CHAPTER 4

The Knife Edge of Experience

The beauty of the world is Christ's tender smile for us, coming through matter.
SIMONE WEIL

Much of our life we are trying to connect the dots, to pierce the heart of reality to see what is good, true, and beautiful for us. We want something lasting and transcendent.[1] We often look in shallow waters, however. Since the Enlightenment of the seventeenth and eighteenth centuries, we have been satisfied with facts, clear evidence, objective science, or things provable by that one excellent discipline and method called science. The hope is that science gives us objective truth; religion, however, gives us personal meaning or personal truth. They should not be seen as contraries.

How we search, however, will determine what we find or even want to find. I suggest that we should be searching primarily in the universal and wise depths of recurring symbols, metaphors, and sacred stories, which is where humans can find deep and lasting meaning—or personal truth. That is what we mean by the Perennial Tradition and why George Bernard Shaw said, "There is only one religion, and there are then a thousand forms of it." The best religious metaphors, like resurrection, assert not just a truth held by Christianity (1 Corinthians 15) but a universal truth too. (Don't panic, fellow Christians. I am not denying the bodily resurrection of Jesus by calling it also a "metaphor"; in fact, quite the contrary. Please read on.)

Metaphor is the only possible language available to religion because it alone is honest about Mystery. The underlying messages that different religions and denominations use are often in strong agreement, but they use different images to communicate their own experience of union with God. That should not shock or disappoint anyone, unless they are still kids shouting, "This is my toy, and the rest of you can't touch it!" Jesus, who is always using metaphors, says, for example, "There are other sheep I have that are not of this fold, and these I have to lead as well. They too listen to my voice" (John 10:16a). He is quite obviously talking metaphorically by calling people sheep. He is also saying that sometimes the outsider to the "flock" hears as well as the insider. Furthermore, he says that he cares about and respects the "other sheep," which means that we should too. These are crucial points, and those who refuse to mine the metaphor will miss them.

Jesus' intention here that there be "only one flock" (John 10:16b) and his later prayer "that all may be one" (John 17:21–23) can be achieved only by overcoming all *otherness*. So Jesus speaks of the "other sheep." The goal is never to overcome all differences, since God already made us different in a hundred thousand ways. *Differences are not the same as otherness, or at least they need not be.* Through clever metaphors such as sheep and flocks, unity and yet differentiation, Jesus resolves the complex philosophical problem of "the one and the many." He uses clever metaphors to teach unclear spiritual truths. He himself calls them parables, and Mark even says, "He would not speak to them except in parables" (4:34), *which means he was willing to risk misunderstanding in hopes that some would get a much deeper understanding* (4:33).

It is impossible to get his strong and important messages here if we do not honor metaphor. Maybe that is exactly why we have missed so much of his core message—just the opposite of what fundamentalists fear. Metaphor is invariably *more* meaning, not less. *Literalism is the lowest and least level of meaning.*

We must never be too tied to our own metaphors as the only possible way to speak the truth, and yet we also need good metaphors to go deep. That is the inherent tension and conflict: only the right symbol dives deep into the good, the true, and the beautiful and retrieves these like pearls from the ocean depths. The right symbol at the right time allows us to move beyond complexity and illusion. Often that which looks like mere symbol is indeed the doorway to all that you really need to know—if you approach it humbly and respectfully. *How else could an always available God be always available?* It cannot depend on having a college education or even a common education, but on a simple ability to read the symbolic universe, which some ancients seem to have done much better than we do.[2]

But do not confuse "humbly and respectfully" with an attitude that is lightweight, saccharine, or ephemeral. Wisdom teachers would say exactly the contrary is true. To see in such a way is the hard work of keeping all inner spaces open at the same time:

mind, heart, and body at the same time. It is at the center of all authentic spirituality and does not happen easily or without *paying respectful and nonegocentric attention to something* — which I would call prayer. Such prayer is perhaps rare, although I hope not.

This must have been what the Cistercian monk, Thomas Merton, was thinking when he saw the smiling, reclining Buddha in Sri Lanka almost at the end of his life and wrote: "Now I have seen and I have pierced through the surface and have got beyond the shadow and the disguise."[3] We are all trying to get beyond the shadow and the disguise of every metaphor, every symbol, every verbal formulation to knock on the hard and true — and wonderful — reality that is underneath mere words. As with Merton, it takes much of our lives and not a knee-jerk reaction to anything. That is my deep desire here. I am not a deconstructionist but a reconstructionist. I love to tell people that *the opposite of contemplation is not action — it is reaction.* Early and quick reaction is almost always egocentric and self-referential.

Both atheists and fundamentalists appear to still be on this side of the shadow and the disguise. They both invariably link to a narrowed-down and literal view of reality and seldom understand metaphor.

They think that symbols do not contain substance, and so they dismiss religious symbols as being wrong, superficial, untrue, unscientific, or "just a symbol." Their literalism strips reality down to a thin floorboard on which they want to walk and feel secure, but it is no longer a shining dance floor, much less a floor on which there is room for everyone to join in the dance.

We live and move in an entirely symbolic universe. Symbols are in fact the only solid way to experience substance. (The Greek root *sym-bolon* means "a throwing together.") True symbols somehow are the thing itself. Our mind throws together meanings largely without realizing we are even doing it. Poets, artists, and storytellers have always known this, and now scientists are honest enough to realize that they too need metaphors to point to reality (for example, black holes, string theory, and the big bang). Without new symbols, which are sometimes also words, unconscious meanings never break through to consciousness, and the invisible has no way of becoming visible. We remain bored and boring. *We do not experience our experiences*—and there is surely no knife edge to our experiences that cuts us open and lances our wounds or refines our happiness.

Symbols allow us to reframe, reorganize, and reset the core meanings of our lives again and again. Many have called our postmodern world "a crisis of meaning," a world where things do not mean anything. It is very lonely in such a universe. Humans cannot live happily without meaning—and ever deeper meaning. Symbols have the power to give meaning—the meanings we wake up for each morning. Religion should be a master at such *mining for meaning*.

Why else do we read novels, have belabored conversations, go to movies, or have sex? Is it not to seek an answer to that most human of questions: "What does this thing called my life mean?" Or, "What does it all mean?" Our answers determine what we actually live and die for (family, spouse, country, God, loyal friendship, love, money). Without meaning we are surely less than human and deeply discontented. Most meaning is largely preconceptual and not subject to words, and in that sense it is nonrational, but meaning lies in wait to appear and grab onto the right symbol in the right moment. We see a sunset, and it mirrors something already inside us that is just waiting to be joyful. We look at Picasso's *Guernica*, and we know and feel the absurdity and terror of war.

At such a moment, we normally feel more alive, connected, and authentic, even if it is sadness that we feel. The inner self is expressed, the inner breath is exhaled, and the inner and outer worlds meet. The universal response is relief and satisfaction. The Greeks call it *katharsis*, or emotional cleansing. The Catholics call it *sacrament*. The world makes sense again, at least for a while. As you grow in seeing, everything becomes symbolic, and you want to write poetry or paint a picture that shows what you are seeing, which is always deeper than mere external appearance. Jesus' words to doubting, probing Thomas take on a whole new meaning: "How happy those who know more than they can see" (John 20:29 in my paraphrase).

Natural symbols, like trees, water, animals, or human nudity, are somehow universal metaphors and work on everybody, even if it is in different ways. Such metaphors "carry us beyond," which is the exact Greek meaning of the word (*meta-phore*). Good religion should be a master at metaphor, carrying us across and beyond. We know, for example, that God is not a "person" in the way we understand human persons, and yet using that word makes any "personal" give-and-take with the Divine possible. I presume that God does not have human, physical emotions, but saying that God "delights" in creation is the only way I can register God's positive engagement with the world of things and creatures. "Person" and "delight" are good and needed metaphors to open up the real thing that many of us call God. Symbols bring things from the hidden unconscious to consciousness, where they can be operative. To say symbols are not true or metaphors are not "real" is just stupid. Sorry if that seems unkind! We live and die for our symbols, because *psychic reality is also reality*!

Religion knew the truth of metaphor and symbol for almost all of history until the past few hundred years, and especially until the wrongly named Enlightenment in the seventeenth and eighteenth centuries. Then we started confusing rational and provable with real. We actually regressed and went backward. In trying to defend its ground in the face of rationalism and scientism, religion tried to become "rational" itself and lost its alternative consciousness, which many of us call contemplation. It's as though we tried to deal with Mystery with the entirely wrong "software." We lost access to the higher levels of consciousness, the transrational, the transpersonal, the transcendent itself. Most tragic, *we lost most inner experience of our own outer belief systems*. That is the heart of religion's problem today, and it is indeed a deep and serious problem for upcoming generations. My generation took the symbols too literally, and now the following generation is just throwing them all out as useless. We are both losing.

It might surprise you, but both religious fundamentalism and atheism are similar in that they are self-contained rational systems. Such a system works if you stay inside its chosen logic and territory. Fundamentalist Christians cannot leave "Texas," fundamentalist Muslims cannot leave "Iraq," fundamentalist Jews cannot leave "Zion," and atheists cannot leave their own institutes and academies. My own Catholic tradition seems not to realize that *Roman* and *catholic* (universal) are actually an oxymoron. As long as each system stays inside its own boundaries, it all works. But not usually in the largest box that Jesus calls the "kingdom [or Reign] of God," or the global world we live in today.

No ego (individual or group ego) ever wants to leave home, it seems. Any notion of universal belonging takes away my specialness, my superiority, and my separateness, which are the precise trademarks of the mental ego. It invariably prefers to calculate instead of to connect. Now you know why people fought and even killed Jesus and why humans love to create controversies instead of find their True Selves.

RESURRECTION

The highly effective symbol that I present in this book might just be the greatest and most beautiful that the human heart seeks and desires. It is resurrection—a universal pattern of the undoing of death. The three Abrahamic religions somehow saw God as the one "who brings the dead to life and calls into being what does not exist" (Romans 4:17). For Christians, this pattern of incarnation, death, and resurrection revealed in "the Christ Mystery" was true long before Jesus of Nazareth, from the very birth and death of the stars to the entire circle of life on this planet. The only Jesus we now know is the risen Christ, the eternal Christ, the Cosmic Christ. *Christ* is simply the word some of us use for "the Body of God."[4] If you do not like the word *Christ*, you can find another, but it is as good as any other to name *God-as-materialized*, which apparently happened about 14.6 billion years ago.

This Eternal (or Cosmic) Christ is God as revealed through every aspect of creation, which is clear in the Scriptures (John 1:1–8; 1 Corinthians 8:6; Colossians

1:15–20, Ephesians 1:3–14; 1 John 1:1–3; Hebrews 1:1–3), and yet is usually not the worldview of most Christians to this day, even those who purport to love Scripture. Most believe in a historical Jesus, but seldom in a Cosmic Christ, as the personalization of the whole universe story (Revelation 21:6, 22:13).[5] Ironically, such true believers in Jesus have made Jesus much smaller than he is or was meant to be. He became their small "tribal god" instead of a "Savior of the World" (John 4:42) or the "Alpha and Omega" of history (Revelation 21:6).

I introduce this notion here to give the full shape of what I mean by the risen Body of Christ but also to illustrate what we have missed out on by not taking seriously our own human experience. St. Anthony of the Desert (251–356) saw it rather clearly and prophetically in the first centuries: "God is gathering us out of all regions till he can make *resurrection of our own hearts from the very earth* [emphasis added], and teach us that we are all of one substance, and members of one another; for the one who loves his neighbor loves God, and the one who loves God, loves his own soul."[6] It would be hard to find a more mature reading of the whole Christian message sixteen centuries later. Sometimes it feels as if we have gone backward.

Many Christians fervently believe in Jesus' bodily resurrection but never get to the "the knife edge of experience," as Rosemary Haughton first called it, and allow "the resurrection of their own hearts" or of history itself.[7] The crucified and Risen Christ is a knife edge that can open our lives — and history itself — into a clear and compelling trajectory.

I believe that the full Christ Mystery serves as a map for the entire journey of the True Self from divine conception, to beloved status, through crucifixion, and unto resurrection. Carl Jung, a frequent critic of Christianity, nevertheless said, "What happens in the life of Christ happens always and everywhere," and he called Christ "the Archetype of the Self."[8] I deeply believe that is true, and I also know that being a Christian today does not demand that you walk this map or recognize this deep pattern to reality. It is too often just a club to join. Indeed, many non-Christians see it, honor it, and live it much better than those who claim to be true believers. You have not been to Russia just because you have a correct map of Russia, and you can fully experience Russia without ever owning the map. But the Christ Mystery is still a good map.

When I use the word *resurrection*, I am not talk-ing about temperamental optimism, not a big Jesus miracle, not a proof that Christianity is the true religion, and I am not encouraging whistling in the dark, or even affirming that there is life after death. I am talking about something much more constant and universal than any of these. If you can see in a mind and heart and body way, you will know that resurrection is a part of almost everything, even the things you love to hate.

Who of us has not been able to eventually see the silver lining in the darkest of life's clouds? There have been too many silver linings in my life to count, and you would think the death/life pattern would be utterly clear to me by now. Yet I still fight and repress my own would-be resurrections, even if just in my mind. I am normally catastrophizing within three seconds of any difficulty or dark emotion. For some damn reason, and I use the cuss word deliberately, we give and get our energy from dark clouds much more than from silver linings. True joy is harder to access and even harder to hold onto than anger or fear. The False Self is energized by problems and by self-created goals almost moment by moment; the True Self (the soul) needs and feeds on a different fuel: *union and contentment itself* and, especially, *deep resonance* (meaning) of any kind.

Once you know that life and death are not two but are part of a whole, you will begin to view reality in a holistic, nonsplit way, and that will be the change that changes everything. It is the initial birth of nondual consciousness. No one can teach you this. Even Jesus had to walk it on his own, which is the only meaning of God "requiring" his death of him. Jesus calls this goal the "destiny" of the "Human One" (Mark 8:31), and he seems to very clearly know that he is a stand-in for all of us (Mark 10:39) — much more than he ever walks around saying, "I am God"! The only person Jesus ever calls a "devil" is Peter, when he tries to oppose this central message (Matthew 16:23) of death and resurrection.

THE DANCE OF BREATH AND CLAY

This whole process of living, dying, and then living again starts with Yahweh "breathing into clay," which becomes "a living being" (Genesis 2:7) called *Adam* ("of the earth"). The point is that a drama is forever set in motion between breath and what appears to be mere clay (humus = human = *adamah*). Matter and spirit are forever bound together; divine and mortal forever interpenetrate and manifest one another. The Formless One forever takes on form as "Adam" (and in Jesus "the new Adam"), and then takes us back to the Formless One once again *as each form painfully surrenders the small self that it has been for a while.* "I am returning to take you with me, so that where I am you also may be" (John 14:3), says Jesus. The changing of forms is called resurrection, and the return is called ascension, although to us it just looks like death.

Buddhists are looking at the same Mystery from a different angle when they say, "Form is emptiness, and emptiness is form," and then all forms eventually return to formlessness (spirit or "emptiness") once again. This is observable and needs no specific religious label as such. Christians call it incarnation → death → resurrection → ascension, but it is about all of us, and surely all of creation, coming forth as individuals and then going back into God, into the Ground of all Being. That cyclical wholeness should make us unafraid of all death and uniquely able to appreciate life. "To God, all people are in fact alive," as Jesus put it (Luke 20:38). We are just in different stages of that aliveness—one of which looks and feels like deadness.

As hidden as the True Self has been from the False Self, so also has the Risen Christ been hidden from most of history. Not surprisingly, we cannot see what we were not told to look for or told to expect. If we were told to look, it was for some divine object outside ourselves instead of realizing that the divine object is also within us. This is the staggering change of perspective that the Gospel was meant to achieve and what I hope to accomplish in this book. This realization is the heart of all religious transformation (*transformare* = to change forms).

The Risen Christ represents the final perspective of every True Self: a human-divine one that is looking out at God from itself—and yet knowing that it is God-in-you seeing God-who-is-also-beyond-you—*and enjoying both yourself and God as good and as united*. Nothing I am trying to say in this book is probably any better or more important than that. It should and could change your life.

OUR DESTINATION

Resurrection is incarnation come to its logical and full conclusion. It fully demonstrates that this world, this flesh, this physicality is part of the eternal truth and forever matters to God. Again, the early church seemed to get this much more than we do. Read, for example, St. Irenaeus and St. Athanasius in their classic texts from the second and fourth centuries.[9] *Resurrection* is saying that matter and spirit have been working together from the first moment of the big bang. Resurrection is not a miracle to be proven; it is a manifestation of the wholeness that we are all meant to experience, even in this world—not time as "chronological moments of endless duration" *but time as momentous and revealing the whole.*[10] When "time comes to a fullness" (Mark 1:15) as in a moment of love, childbirth, union, peaceful death, or beauty, you have then experienced a moment of eternal life. Resurrection is when one moment reveals the meaning of all moments. Without such moments, it will either be very hard for you to imagine resurrection or, conversely, you will long for it like no one else, which is the concise meaning of the virtue of hope.

The Risen Christ is the standing icon of humanity in its final and full destiny. He is the pledge and guarantee of what God will do with all of our crucifixions. At last, we can meaningfully live with hope. It is no longer an absurd or tragic universe. *Our hurts now become the home for our greatest hopes.* Without such implanted hope, it is very hard not to be cynical, bitter, and tired by the second half of our lives.

It is no accident that Luke's Resurrection account in the Gospel has Jesus saying, "I am not a ghost! I have flesh and bones, as you can see" (24:39–41). To Thomas he says, "Put your finger in the wounds!" (John 20:27). In other words, "I am human!" — which means to be wounded and resurrected at the same time. He returns to his physical body, and yet he is now unlimited by space or time and is without any regret or recrimination — while still, ironically, carrying his wounds. (That they do not disappear is telling.) It was quite a feat to communicate this whole message in such a subtle and refined way, which is precisely the power of symbol. "Our wounds are our glory," as Lady Julian of Norwich puts it, is the utterly counterintuitive message of the risen Jesus.

The major point is that Jesus has not left the human sphere; he is revealing the goal, the fullness, and the purpose of humanity itself, which is "that we are able to share in the divine nature" (2 Peter 1:4), even in this wounded and wounding world. Yes, resurrection is saying something about Jesus, but it is also saying a lot about us, which is even harder to believe. It is saying that we also are larger than life, Being Itself, and therefore made for something good, united, and beautiful. Our code word for that is *heaven*.

When we take the Resurrection symbol and its substance absolutely seriously, it moves us far beyond the stripped-down literal meaning where both atheists and fundamentalists flounder. It does not even have to mean "eternally enduring life in our current form or even in the future"; instead, it might also mean "a present life of eternal significance." But surely it means a life of goodness and love, both of which have an eternal quality to them. For many of us, it is a life of "adopted" sonship and daughterhood, whereby we share in Jesus' divine inheritance or are "heirs of the same promise," the metaphors that Paul effectively uses. I am so saddened that much of Christian history that has read these same metaphors seems to have had so little inner experience to know that it is actually true—and true for them.

No matter what your definition, we all want resurrection in some form. And I do believe "the raising up of Jesus" (which is the correct theological way to say it because it was a relational meaning between Jesus and God, and not a self-generated "I can do this") is still a potent, focused, and compelling statement about *what God is still and forever doing with the universe and with humanity*. Science strongly confirms this statement today—more than ever before—but with different metaphors and symbols, like condensa-tion, evaporation, hibernation, sublimation, the four seasons, the life cycles of everything from salmon to galaxies, and even the constant death and birth of stars from the exact same stardust. *God appears to be resurrecting everything all the time.* It is nothing to "believe in" as much as it is something to observe and be taught by.

Many do believe in the bodily resurrection, as I do too, but in a way that asks little except a mere intellectual assertion of a religious doctrine. We can go much further than that. I choose to believe in some kind of bodily resurrection because it localizes the whole Mystery in this material and earthly world and in our own bodies, the only world we know and the world that God created and loves. As is often the case, the religious tradition usually intuits things correctly, even if it often states those intuitions in language and symbols that many people then fight against. When we can look behind the language and symbols, we can choose to keep the lovely baby even if we don't like the bathwater that it swims in.

We all want to know that this wonderful thing called life is going somewhere, and somewhere good. Maybe even somewhere likely! It is going to someplace good because it came from someplace good too — a place of "original blessing" instead of a place of "original sin."[11] "I know where I came from and where I am going," Jesus says, "but you do not" (John 8:14). The Alpha and the Omega of history have to match somehow, or our lives have no natural arc, trajectory, or organic meaning. If the original incarnation was and is true, then resurrection is both inevitable and irreversible. If the big bang was the external starting point of the eternal Christ Mystery, then we know this eternal logos is leading creation somewhere good, and it is not a chaotic or meaningless universe. No one taught this better than the Jesuit mystic and paleontologist Teilhard de Chardin. Read him if you want a truly cosmic and hopeful vision of things. In perfect timing, he fell dead on the streets of the secular city of New York on Easter Sunday morning in 1955.

The only rub, and it is a big one, is that transformation and "crucifixion" must intervene in between life and Life. Loss always precedes renewal in the physical and biological universe. This is where we all fumble, falter, and fight. Someone needs to personally lead the way, model the path, and say it is a "necessary suffering." Otherwise we will not trust this counterintuitive path. For Christians, this model and exemplar is Jesus.

Since life energy hovered over "the chaos" of creation from the very start (Genesis 1:1–2), the Catholic tradition spoke of the Holy Spirit as "uncreated grace." It is uncreated because the spirit is an inherent part of the unfolding of God's grace since the very beginning of time (Romans 8:18–25). Hope was implanted in creation from the start. Salvation is promised from the inside out and from the beginning forward. Now we call it evolution. The great unfolding of God's Mystery "infolds" all the previous stages, and nothing is wasted or discarded—not even evil, death, or sin (this is precisely why the Bible includes those disappointing stories of murder, rape, deceit, and war).

Someone is going somewhere with this whole thing called life. *Why would the Creator create a universe where all the parts grow and develop but not the whole?* God is without doubt a great risk taker, and probably that explains the endless and bizarre displays of life that we see on this earth. God is clearly into freedom, imagination, and creativity. Look at nature: we end up with every conceivable shape and color of jellyfish, desert kangaroos that turn their urine back into liquid to nurse their young, and twenty-five hundred types of cicadas, some of which appear only every seventeen years. Who is this God? You could call God *unfettered resurrection*! Humans, by contrast, are preoccupied with stability, efficiency, and control, even if it means boredom and death.

Once you know there is an implanted and positive direction to creation, you can go with the primary flow (faith); eventually you will learn to rest there (hope), and finally you will actually live there most of the day (love). You are home at last in an inherently sacred universe.

LOVE AND TRUTH

The first principle of great spiritual teachers is rather constant here: *only love can be entrusted with the Big Truth*. All other attitudes will murder and mangle truthfulness. Humans must first find the unified field of love and then start their thinking from that point. All prayer disciplines are somehow trying to get head and heart and body to work as one, and that changes thinking entirely. "The concentration of attention in the heart—this is the starting point of prayer," says St. Theophane the Recluse, the nineteenth-century Russian mystic. Any other "handler" of your experience, including the rational mind or even mere intellectual theology, eventually distorts and destroys the beauty and healing power of Big Truth. One of my favorite fathers of the church, Evagrius Ponticus (345–399), said that you could not be a theologian unless you knew how to pray, and only people who prayed could be theologians. This is surely true.

Perhaps the second principle is that truth is on some level always beautiful — and healing — to those who honestly want truth. Big Truth cannot be angry, antagonistic, or forced on anyone, or it will inherently distort the message. John Duns Scotus, in good Franciscan style, taught that the primary moral category was beauty itself, or what he called "the harmony of goodness."[12] The good, the united, and the true in this world will always be somehow beautiful too, and beautiful souls will recognize it immediately.

The anger and mutual disrespect that I find among both conservative and progressive Christians today is really quite disturbing. It feels aligned much more with political ideologies of Right and Left than any immersion in the beautiful love of God. Jihadism and Zionism have become the death knell of any remaining beauty in religion for many sincere seekers all over the world. It is all so sad that we could regress so far in the name of God, who wants only to lead us forward.

The good, the true, and the beautiful are always their own best argument for themselves—by themselves—and in themselves. Such beauty, or inner coherence, is a deep inner knowing that both evokes the soul and even pulls the soul into its oneness. Incarnation is beauty, and beauty always needs to be incarnate. Anything downright "good," anything that shakes you with its "trueness," and anything that sucks you into its beauty does not just educate you; it transforms you. True religion proceeds like the twelve-step program—"by attraction and not promotion." Simone Weil said it so well: "There is only one fault, only one: our inability to feed upon light."[13]

For me, the Resurrection is a big neon sign that keeps alluring and inviting history forward toward its certain conclusion. The Risen Christ is, as Teilhard de Chardin tried to describe it, the divine lure, a blinking, brilliant light set as the Omega point of time and history that keeps reminding us that love, not death, is the eternal thing. Love, which is nothing more than endless life, is luring us forward, because *love is what we also and already are* and we are drawn to the fullness of our own being. Remember, "Like knows Like" and like an electromagnetic force, it is drawing the world into a fullness of love. We will finally have no choice. Love always wins.

In the practical order of experience, *self-knowledge and God knowledge will be experienced as the same knowing and will proceed forward in parallel fashion.* There is a clear affinity between human intimacy and divine intimacy, which we will discuss in Chapter Eight. *How you know anything is how you know everything.* With that, we are getting much deeper into our diamond mine. Paul says the same: "Then you shall know as fully as you are known" (1 Corinthians 13:12). And finally John (1 John 3:2) transfers it all to the end of time: "All we know is that when it is revealed—we shall all be like him." And "the life you already have is hidden with Christ in God" (Colossians 3:3).

Your experience of your deepest and truest self and your deepest experiences of God will prove one another right—and prove one another good. Neither of them will go deep or true, however, without the knife edge of your own honest experience, which will cut you wide open in both directions. You have nothing to be afraid of as long as you do not start or end with fear, accusation, or judgment.

"The word of God is something alive and active. It cuts like a two-edged sword, but more finely yet . . . interpreting the secret emotions and thoughts of the heart" (Hebrews 4:12). That is indeed the knife edge of experience.

CHAPTER 5

Thou Art That

The place which God takes in our soul he will never vacate, for in us is his home of homes, and it is the greatest delight for him to dwell there.... The soul who contemplates this is made like the one who is contemplated.

LADY JULIAN OF NORWICH, *SHOWINGS*

On that day, you will know that you are in me and I am in you.

JOHN 14:20

"That day" that John refers to in the second epigraph has been a long time in coming, yet it has been the enduring message of every great religion in history. It *is* the Perennial Tradition. Yet union with God is still considered esoteric, mystical, a largely moral matter, and possible only for a very few, as if God were playing hard to get. Nevertheless, divine and thus universal union is still the core message and promise—the whole goal and the entire point of all religion.

Place does not exist except in God. There is no time outside God. God is the beauty in all beauty. Those who allow divine friendship enjoy divine friendship, and it is almost that simple. You are that which you are looking for, and that is why you are looking for it. God's life and love flow through you as soon as *you* are ready to allow it. That is the core meaning of faith — to dare to trust that God could, will, and does have an eternal compassion toward you. Everyone who asked Jesus to heal them or help them had somehow made that simple act of trust that he cared — and so the flow happened and they were healed. No other preconditions were ever required. It is really rather shocking.

If you are seeking the divine, you have already made contact with the divine in yourself. If you have not made contact with the divine in yourself, you will likely be bored with any notion of spiritual search. If you have, you will seek and find it everywhere. The modern divine-human divorce seems to be on the grounds of both "incompatibility" and "irreconcilable" differences. Religion itself must bear most of the responsibility for causing this divorce by, in effect, increasing the distance between God and humanity instead of proudly announcing that the problem is already solved and the perceived gap has been overcome from the very beginning: "Before the world was made, he chose us" (Ephesians 1:4).

Jesus fully accepted and enjoyed his divine-human status. "I and the Father are one," he said (John 10:30), which was shocking to his Jewish contemporaries, for he looked just like one of them, and apparently they did not like themselves. No wonder they called it blasphemy and picked up stones to kill him (John 10:33). You do know, I hope, that it is formally incorrect for Christians to simply say, "Jesus is God," although that is the way they do think. But it misses the major point and goal of the whole incarnation. Jesus does not equal God per se, which is for us the Trinity. Jesus, much better and more correctly, is *the union between God and the human*. That is a third something—which in fact we are invited to share in. Once we made Jesus *only* divine, we ended up being *only* human, and the whole process of human transformation ground to a halt. That is the way the dualistic mind works, I am very sad to say.[1] For some of you, these paragraphs could be the most important in this book.

When we tried to understand Jesus outside the dynamism of the Trinity, we did not do him or ourselves any favor. Jesus never knew himself or operated as an independent "I" but only as a "thou" in relationship to his Father and the Holy Spirit, which he says in a hundred different ways. The "Father" and the "Holy Spirit" are a relationship to Jesus. *God* is a verb more than a noun. God is love, which means relationship itself (1 John 4:7–8).

Christianity lost its natural movement and momentum—out from that relationship and back into that relationship—when it pulled Jesus out of the Trinity.[2] It killed what is the exciting inner experience and marginalized the mystics who really should be center stage. Jesus is the model and metaphor for all of creation that is all being drawn into this flow of love, and thus he always says, "Follow me!" and, "I shall return to take you with me, so that where I am, you may be also" (John 14:3). The concrete, historical body of Jesus represents the universal Body of Christ that "God has loved before the foundation of the world" (John 17:24). He is the stand-in for all of us. The Jesus story is the universe story, in other words. His union with God that Jesus never doubts, he hands on to us—to never doubt. (Quite simply, this is what it means to "believe" in Jesus.)

The spiritual wisdom of divine union is first beautifully expressed in writing in the Vedas (the oldest source of Hinduism, around three thousand years old), and it is one of its "grand pronouncements." The phrase in Sanskrit is *Tat Tvam Asi*, which is a thought so condensed that I am going to list all likely translations, and know that however you hear it, it is still true and is the Perennial Tradition of religion:

- YOU are That!
- You ARE what you seek!
- THOU art That!
- THAT you are!
- You are IT!

The meaning of this saying is that the True Self, in its original, pure, primordial state, is wholly or partially identifiable or even identical with God, the Ultimate Reality that is the ground and origin of all phenomena. That which you long for, you also are. In fact, that is where the longing comes from.

Longing for God and longing for our True Self are the same longing. And the mystics would say that it is God who is even doing the longing in us and through us (that is, through the divine indwelling, or the Holy Spirit). God implanted a natural affinity and allurement between himself and all of his creatures. The limited and the limitless would otherwise be incapable of union; the finite and the infinite could never be reconciled into one.

Religion has only one job description: how to make one out of two. For Christians, that is "the Christ Mystery," whereby we believe God overcame the gap from God's side. God does all the work, the heavy lifting, and always initiates the longing. Some called it "prevenient grace," which makes the point quite well.[3] The deepest human need and longing is to overcome the separateness, the distance from what always seems "over there" and "beyond me," like a perfect lover, a moment of perfection in art, music, or dance, and surely a transcendent God.

Yet God is saying in all incarnations that "I am not totally Other. I have planted some of me in all things that long for reunion." It is mimicked and mirrored in erotic desire and the sexual pairing of all animals, which is why the Song of Songs, Rumi, Hafiz, Kabir, and John of the Cross could use only highly erotic images to communicate their mysticism. Absolute otherness will create only absolute alienation. (Add to that any notion of God as petty, angry, or torturing, and the mystical journey is over.) So God created human sameness and compassion in the human Jesus to overcome this tragic gap. God-in-you seeks and loves God, like a homing device that never turns off.

It should be no scandal or surprise that sex is so obsessive, scary, and fascinating. It is the most dramatic way that we all try to overcome our separateness. The French phrase for that return to separateness after sex is *la petite mort*, or "the little death." The good, the true, and the beautiful are always still beyond me, outside me, and above me. We all seem to feel incapable and unworthy of perfection, and after every moment of experienced union, we sadly fall back into the more familiar distance. Yet we keep trying, and that is good. Even our clumsy amorous attempts give us a taste and a promise now and then, and there is not much point in always calling them "sins." God is not going to waste anything and will use everything, even our clumsy amorous attempts, to bring us into union with God and ourselves.

Re-ligio ("rebinding, re-ligamenting") is not doing its job if it only reminds you of your distance, your unworthiness, your sinfulness, and your inadequacy before God's greatness. Whenever religion actually increases the gap, it becomes antireligion instead. I am afraid we have lots of antireligion in all denominations. I always figured that was the meaning of the very first devil Jesus met and had to exorcise; notice it was living in the synagogue itself (Mark 1:21–28). So I am not talking about the devils of secularism, scientism, or atheism. I am talking about the common blockages and boundary markers inside religion itself—anything that deliberately increases the gap between my unworthiness and the "supreme majesty" of God — the exact and very gap that Jesus came to deny and undo.

Such *gap-creating* between God and creation is truly diabolical (*dia balein*, Greek, to throw apart), and he calls it so: "Alas for you hypocrites! You shut up the kingdom of heaven in peoples' faces, neither going in yourself, nor allowing others to go in who want to" (Matthew 23:13). I would surely be afraid and hesitant to say that if he had not said it first. Jesus said it first (and then Paul did) by warning us against any notion of religion as mere laws, requirements, or purity codes. Yet that is where most religion is to this day. We pulled Jesus inside our "conventional wisdom" and seldom allowed him to be the teacher of alternative wisdom that he always has been.[4]

THE COMMON DETOURS AND DEAD ENDS

Moralism is the common substitute and counterfeit for mysticism in almost all religions. Moralism (as opposed to healthy morality) is our reliance on largely arbitrary purity codes, magic rituals, and "requirements" for our supposed enlightenment, "salvation," or any form of superiority. Every group and individual relies on moralism in its early stages. We look for something behavioral to *externally do or not do* rather than undergo a radical transformation *of our very mind and heart*. I guess that would be *la grande mort*, or too big a death. Mature religion is about change, not little changes. But little changes and adjustments here and there are so much easier.

Paul states the contrast perfectly when he says to the early Jewish Christians: "It does not matter whether one is circumcised or not, what matters is that you become a whole new creation" (Galatians 6:16). And remember that circumcision was as important for Jews as baptism is for Christians. Divine union is not the same as personal perfection; they are quite different paths. It was St. Irenaeus of Lyon, called the first Christian theologian, who said, "The Son of God was made man so that man might become sons of God."[5] That, brothers and sisters, despite his sexist use of words, is the whole point — not circumcision or baptism. Think of the Christian denominations that have divided over the who, when, where, how, what words, how much water, and by whom of baptism. To my knowledge, Abraham, Moses, St. Joseph, and the Blessed Virgin Mary were never baptized. They were just transformed.

By *moralism*, I mean any technique or ritual of private perfection. Moral achievement invariably becomes a carrot on a stick—a largely arbitrary but only half-true goal that is always a bit beyond you. It makes any experience of union largely impossible, and that is its problem (as Romans and Galatians make resoundingly clear). You can now be independently "good" without the love and mercy of God, or anybody else for that matter. The big moral issues change from century to century and culture to culture. Once it was "eating with pagans" (Galatians 2:12). By the early Middle Ages, it was usury (taking interest on loans, which we have no problem with now), Catholics still confess "missing Mass on Sunday" more than any other sin (when that is not even in the same category of many of the evils we are easily condoning), and today the moral issue is abortion and gay marriage. What will it be in the next century?

The moralistic agenda is revealed by the fact that one is never quite pure enough, holy enough, moral enough, or enough of an insider to the proper group. This process of "sin management" has kept us clergy in enduring business—and it must bore God to death, considering the weak historic ratings and results from all of our moralizing. (I have been pickpocketed twice in my life, both in pious Catholic countries: on the bus to St. Peter's in Rome and in front of a Marian shrine in the Philippines. I never felt safer than on the streets of India and Japan.)

In a moralistically oriented religious group, there are always clear outsiders to be kept clearly outside. Hiding inside this false moral purity are things like slavery; sexism; the greed of Christian emperors, clergy, and citizens; pedophilia; national conquest; oppression of Native cultures. Greed and war are easily overlooked. That is no exaggeration if you read church history. We have not largely been dealing with any deep Jesus spirituality up to now but what some impatiently call "churchianity." We Catholics had to canonize saints because they were the rare exception instead of the norm. The New Testament, in contrast, regularly calls all Christians "the saints."

The good news of an incarnational religion, a Spirit-based morality, is that you are not motivated by outside reward or punishment but actually by looking out from inside the Mystery yourself. So carrots are neither needed nor helpful. "It is God, who for his own loving purpose, puts both the will and the action into you" (Philippians 2:13). It is not our rule-following behavior but our actual identity that needs to be radically changed. This is a major change of position and vantage point. You do things because they are true, not because you have to or you are afraid of punishment. Henceforth you are not so much *driven from without* (the False Self method) as you are *drawn from within* (the True Self method). The generating motor is inside you now instead of a whip or a threat outside.

Before transformation, you pray *to* God. After transformation you pray *through* God, as the Christian liturgies always say: "*Through* Christ our Lord. Amen!" Before radical conversion, you look for God as if God were an object like all other objects. After conversion (*con-vertere*, to turn around or to turn with), you look out from God with eyes other than your own. As the Dominican, Meister Eckhart put it in one of his *Sermons*, "The eye through which I see God is the same eye through which God sees me; my eye and God's eye are one eye, one seeing, one knowing, one love."[6] All humans are doing is allowing God to "complete the circuit" within us — until we both see from the same perspective.

Every viewpoint is a view from a point, and our vantage point is utterly changed by God. Only then is the gap overcome, and quite effectively I might add. When we can see in this way, we know we are now living from our True Self. When your very "I" changes, the rest of your life will fall into place—a mighty fine place too. A fourth-century Syrian mystic called Pseudo-Macarius said that after we have been found by God, we are "nothing but gazing." By the second and third weeks of my Lenten hermitages, I take long walks. I stop thinking and even feeling, and I just look, and see, everything—in exact color, shape, texture, and all inside of utter gratitude and harmony. It is wide-eye seeing without commentary. It is pure awareness and not "thinking" as such. Then I can write and have something to say from the pulpit.

A MYSTERY OF PARTICIPATION

"I have seen the Totality, received not in essence, but by participation. When you light a flame from a flame, it is the same flame that you receive," says St. Symeon the New Theologian (949–1022). He represents the best of the older Orthodox Christian tradition and yet he is totally contemporary too. He is one of the few saints of whom it was commonly said that he "knew God face to face" like Moses (Exodus 33:11) and Jacob (Genesis 32:31)—neither of them moral paragons, by

the way. The consistently flawed biblical characters, whom God nevertheless uses for divine purposes, should have shown us that participation with God and perfect morality are not the same thing. In fact, Meister Eckhart goes so far as to say, "A human's best chance of finding God is to look in the very place where they abandoned God."[7] God is waiting right there in the experience of your falling.

Some of the most exciting and fruitful theology today is being described as the "turn toward participation."[8] Religion as participation is a rediscovery of the Perennial Tradition that Plotinus, Gottfried Leibniz, Alan Watts, Aldous Huxley, and so many saints and mystics have spoken of in their own ways. It constantly recognizes that *we are a part of something more than we are observing something*. The turn toward participation now sees that most of religious and church history has been largely preoccupied with religious ideas, about which you could be wrong or right. When it is all about ideas, you did not have to be a part of "it"; you just needed to talk correctly about "it." You never had to dive in and illustrate that spiritual proof is only in the pudding. You never have to actually go to Russia; you just need a correct map of Russia and the willingness to say, "My map is better than your map," or, more commonly, "Mine is the only true map," without offering any corroborating evidence that your map has in fact gotten you there.

The spiritual question is this: Does one's life give any evidence of an encounter with God? Does this encounter bring about in you any of the things that Paul describes as the "fruits" of the Spirit: "love, joy, peace, patience, kindness, goodness, trustfulness, gentleness, and self control" (Galatians 5:22)? Is the person or the group after this encounter different from its surroundings, or does it reflect the predictable cultural values and biases of its group?

Or, even worse, does your religion spend much of its time defining and deciding who *cannot* participate? When there is not much to enjoy from the inside, all you can do is keep yourself above and apart from others. Many groups still "forbid under pain of sin" worshiping God in another denominational space. Please. Such religion is nothing but groupthink and boundary marking, and is not likely to lead you to any deep encounter with God. Such smallness will never be ready or eager for true greatness.

If God is for you a tyrant, an eternal torturer, or with a smaller heart than most people you know, why would you want to be intimate, spend time with, or even "participate" with such a God? As Helen Keller once said, "I sometimes fear that much religion is man's despair at *not* finding God." Most groups picked a few moral positions to give themselves a sense of worthiness and discipline, or a few sacraments to "attend," but loving and even erotic divine union still largely remained a secret or foolish to imagine. "I don't have time for the mystics; we are running a church here," a bishop once told me. I'm not kidding. And he was not a bad man or a bad bishop, but he was an outsider to the very Mystery that he talked about in the church he was "running."

Playing king of the hill always overrides any actual party on the hill. Jesus makes that very point in his several parables of the wedding party or the great banquet (see Luke 14:7–24 or Matthew 22:1–10). Parties are about participation, not legislation. If there is not room for one more at your party, you are a very poor host. And God is not a poor host.

Participation has not been the strong suit or primary position in any of the three monotheistic religions up to now, except among some subsets of Hasidic Jews, Hesychastic Orthodox, the Sufi Muslims, lots of Catholic mystics, and the many individuals who would have fit into any of these groups if they had known about them. Protestantism as a whole seldom moved toward any notion of real or universal participation, although many, many Protestant individuals did. As in Catholicism, many learned to keep officially quiet and practiced their "generous orthodoxy" on the sly and on the side. In the Franciscans, we always say, "It was easier to ask for forgiveness than to ask for permission." Don't expect a lot of freedom or permission from most religious people, but thank God, the Gospel requires them to give you forgiveness.

The "participatory turn" is learning from concrete practices, personal disciplines, and interactive dialogues that change the seer and allow and encourage the encounter itself. Many Christians today are rediscovering prayer beads, prayer of quiet, icons, contemplative sits, Taize chants, charismatic prayer, walking meditation, Zen chores, extended silence, solitude, and disciplined spiritual direction. Up to now, you could have a doctorate in theology as a Catholic or Protestant and not really know how to pray or even enjoy prayer (experienced union), although you could recommend it officially to others and maybe even define it. Now we need to personally live it.

PARTICIPATION AND CONSCIOUSNESS

Both the work of German philosopher Karl Jaspers and the English scholar Owen Barfield have given me a schema for understanding what seems to have happened, and how we actually moved away from any deep participatory experience into a recent "desert of nonparticipation," as Barfield calls it.[9]

Roughly before 800 B.C., it seems, most people connected with God and reality through myth, poetry, dance, music, fertility, and nature. Although it was a violent world focused on survival, there is much evidence that many people might have had healthier psyches than we do today. It was still a frightening and dangerous world, but they knew at least that they belonged inside of it for good or for ill. This was called *Pre-axial Consciousness* by Karl Jaspers. They knew they participated in what was still an utterly enchanted universe. This was the preexistent "church that existed since Abel" (once there were at least three!) that St. Augustine and St. Gregory spoke of. Barfield called this "original participation."

What Jaspers calls *Axial Consciousness* emerged worldwide with the Eastern sages, the Jewish prophets, and the Greek philosophers, all around 500 B.C., and laid the foundations of all of the world's religions and major philosophies. It was the birth of systematic and conceptual thought. In the East, it often took the form of the holistic thinking that is found in Hinduism, Taoism, and Buddhism, which allowed people to experience forms of participation with reality, themselves, and the divine. In the West, the Greek genius gave us a kind of Mediated Participation through thought, reason, and philosophy, while many mystics seemed to enjoy real participation, even when it was officially seen as a very narrow gate available to only a few.

On the cusp of East and West, there was a dramatic realization of intimate union and Group Participation with God among the people called Israel. They recognized the individually enlightened person like Moses or Isaiah, but they did something more. The notion of participation was widened to the Jewish group and beyond, at least for many of the Hebrew prophets. The people were being saved; participation was historical and not just individual. The Bible at its best became the salvation of history itself, which is why we have to endure all those "unholy" historical books. Most of the love and the accusation language in the Bible is not addressed to individuals but to Israel as a whole. Yahweh's concern is first of all *societal*; the covenant is with the people of Israel, not individual Jews. It is amazing that we have forgotten or ignored this, which reflects Western hyperindividualism.

Nevertheless, the confluence of the Eastern Semitic mind, Jewish religion, and Greek and Roman influence in Palestine created a matrix into which a new realization could be communicated, and Jesus the Jew soon offered the world Full and Final Participation in his own holistic teaching, which allowed him to speak of true union at all levels: with oneself, with the group, with the neighbor, with the outsider and even the enemy, with Jesus himself, and, through all of these, with God. You have got to know that this is pretty amazing. (To give citations to all of these would amount to quoting much of the New Testament.)

Although this message was periodically enjoyed and taught and is found in Paul's mystical writings, the vast majority of Christians made the Christian religion into the carrot on the stick that I talked about earlier. The desert fathers and mothers, the early Eastern fathers, the early Celts who were outside the empire, some monasteries and hermits, and the constant recurrence of mystics and holy people let us know it was always realized by some. But it was an underground stream and hardly ever the mainline tradition, which tended to be whitewater rapids and fast-food religion. Only contemplatives, whether conscious or "hidden," knew how to get there and return there—with their nondual and inclusive way of processing the moment.

Unfortunately the monumental insights of the Axial period that formed all of us in foundational and good ways began to dry up and wane, descending into the extreme headiness of some Scholastic philosophy (1100–1500), the antagonistic mind of almost all church reformations, and the rational literalism of the Enlightenment. Although the reformations were inevitable, good, and necessary, they also ushered in the "Desert of Nonparticipation," as Barfield called it, where no one belonged, few were at home in this world, and religion at its worst concentrated on excluding, condemning, threatening, judging, exploiting new lands and peoples, and controlling its own members by shame and guilt—on both the Catholic and Protestant sides. Despite exceptions in every nation, church, denomination, group, monastery, and age, we almost totally lost the "alternative processing system," which I would call contemplation. I know this sounds sinister and regressive, but there is plenty of evidence for its truth. Most of it was not conscious, but the product of ignorance, fear, and overreaction. Now the Christian world has produced more atheists, anti-Christians, witch hunts, and secularists than any other region would think possible. How can a society survive when it hates its own religion or the very notion of deep participation?

Jaspers and Barfield, and also Ewert Cousins, each in his own way, foresaw the coming of a II Axial Consciousness, when the best of each era will combine and work together: the prerational, the rational, and the transrational. We live in such a time! In this consciousness, we can now make use of the unique contribution of every era to enjoy intuitive and body knowledge, along with rational critique and deeper synthesis, thus encouraging both intelligent and heartfelt participation "with our whole heart, soul, mind and strength," as Jesus puts it (Mark 12:30).

We are living in a wonderful and blessed time, if you can accept and enjoy this II Axial Age, which is in many ways already upon us. I must admit that there are many signs that it is not "upon us," and in fact, the contrary is the case. Whenever Spirit descends anew, the forces of resistance to it become all the stronger, even in the world religions. Both are surely true in our time. So how can we do our part to further "the work," "the great turning," the "refounding" in our own lifetime? *We must rebuild from the very bottom up, and that means restoring the inherent sacrality of all things — no exceptions — and all the past mistakes must be included as teaching moments and not just something to hate.* We must relink all the links in "the great chain of being."[10]

THE PEARL OF GREAT PRICE

The Greek word *theosis,* often used by the Eastern Fathers of the Church, is probably best translated as "divinization." [11] Although usually taught in the more mystical and Trinitarian Eastern church, it was largely lost in the more practical, carrot-on-the-stick emphasis of the Western church. Every time the Christian church divided or separated, each group lost one half of the Gospel message, and that seems to have been true in the Great Schism of 1054, when the popes of East and West mutually excommunicated one another. The same loss of wholeness happened again in 1517 with the Protestant reformers (Martin Luther, John Calvin, John Knox, and Henry VIII), and again with our split from science at the time of Galileo, and many times since. Almost all of our Judeo-Christian history reflects a split from the feminine, which certainly lost us half of the truth. Both sides always lost something good. This is the very sad result of dualistic thinking, which is incapable of comprehending, much less experiencing, the mystical, nonviolent, or nondual level of anything ("not totally one but not two either"). The contemplative mind should be religion's unique gift to society. It greases the wheels of spiritual evolution.

So let's reintroduce this Gospel "pearl of great price" to the Western church, both Roman and Protestant, and to the secular seeker.[12] As Simone Weil said in various ways, it is much easier to make non-Christians into Christians than it is to make Christians into Christians. Cradle Christians are almost totally preconditioned to the carrot-on-the-stick model.

But lest any Western Catholics think I am dredging up some old condemned heresy, consider this quote from Pope John Paul II in 1995: "The venerable and ancient tradition of the Eastern Churches, that is the teaching of the Cappadocian Fathers on divinization (*theosis*), passed into the tradition of all the Eastern Churches and is part of their common heritage. This can be summarized in the thought already expressed by St. Irenaeus at the end of the second century: 'God passed into man so that man might pass over to God.'"[13] Popes do not speak of such things unless they know they have serious credibility and authority behind them. Pope John was surely acknowledging that the Western church, both Catholic and Protestant, had largely lost its belief in divinization or had even denied its possibility. No wonder we suffer from such universal lack of self-esteem and cultural self-loathing.

The shining and oft-quoted "proof text" here is 2 Peter 1:3–4, where the inspired author says, "By his divine power, God has given us all the things we need for life and for true devotion that allow us to know God himself, who has called us by his own glory and goodness. In this gift God has given us a guarantee of something very great and wonderful. Through this gift *you are sharers in the divine nature itself*." There it is, for those of you who need a Scripture.

Many of the fathers of the church believed in an actual ontological, metaphysical, objective union between humanity and God, which alone would allow Jesus to take us "back with him" into the life of the Trinity (John 17:23–24, 14:3, 12:26). This was how real "participation" was for many in the early church. It

changed people and offered them their deepest identity
and form ("trans-formation"). We had thought our
form was merely human, but Jesus came to tell us
that our actual form is human-divine, just as he is.
He was not much interested in proclaiming himself
the exclusive or exclusionary son of God, but he went
out of his way to communicate an *inclusive* sonship
and daughterhood to the crowds. Paul uses words like
"adopted" (Galatians 4:5) and "coheirs with Christ"
(Romans 8:17) to make the same point.

"Full and Final Participation" was learned from
Jesus, who clearly believed that God was not so much
inviting us into a distant heaven, but inviting us into
himself as friends and coparticipants. Remember, *I am
not talking about a psychological or moral wholeness
in human persons, which is never the case, and why
many dismiss this doctrine—or feel incapable of it*.
I am talking about a divinely implanted "sharing in
the divine nature," which is called the indwelling
spirit or the Holy Spirit (Romans 8:16–17). This is
the substratum on which we must and can build and
rebuild a civilization of life and love. Without it, most
religious pep talks are Platonic idealism and largely
ineffective attempts to inspire and motivate the False

Self. The reason we have to keep coming back to church each Sunday is because last Sunday's message did not work at any deep level.

THE DIVINE INDWELLING

This awesome and even presumptuous message of divinization was supported by Genesis 1:27 and 5:2 where we are told that we are "created in the *image and likeness* of God." Many tomes of theology have been written to clarify this quote, and this was the consensus. "Image" was defined as our *objective* DNA that marked us as creatures of God from the very beginning, before we could do anything right or anything wrong. The divine indwelling was a total gratuitous gift, standing presence, and guarantee; it is the Holy Spirit living within us, sometimes called "uncreated grace." We were the containers, "temples," or recipients of this gift. In a certain sense, it had nothing to do with us, and yet said everything about our core identity. It gave every human being an inherent dignity, which I am calling in this book your True Self and your immortal diamond. This for Christians is "the rock of salvation." The indwelling divine image moves toward fulfillment in each of us, like a slow-release probiotic or supervitamin. This was, without doubt, the "original blessing."

"Likeness" was something else. Likeness was *our personal appropriation and gradual realization* of this utterly free gift of the image of God. We all have the objective same gift, but how we subjectively say yes to it is quite different. Seeing our daily unlikeness to God in ourselves and in others, the practical Western church could not go there. But it all depends on what you pay attention to. The contemplative dimension of the church allowed you to rest in this deeper truth, self, and Mystery.

The more active and extroverted Western church could only see the externals of people as very unlike God, and it paid attention to moral achievements instead of mystical center. The best that Luther could do was offer what he said was "a layer of snow over a pile of manure," while Calvin offered us a starting point of "total depravity" and "predestination of the elect." It is difficult to see that any divinization is possible in such an inherently negative anthropology. How do you rebuild when you are that far in the deficit? In Catholicism, Cardinal Ratzinger called gay people "intrinsically disordered." How can you ever hear the good news if your problem is "intrinsic"? This is actually antievangelism. The West, as a whole, never got the core right but danced around the circumference. Divinization was preserved in the deep stream, never in the upper rapids.

In short, the early Eastern church and the contemplative tradition in the West emphasized image, while the Western church, both Roman and Protestant, largely emphasized likeness. The Western church lost the ground and transformative center; the Eastern church lost the dynamic and cutting edge that moved outward. In the end, we all lost out on "the glory and goodness" of God that 2 Peter speaks of. And so did human and church history. We forgot that the ear cannot say to the eye, "I do not need you" (1 Corinthians 12:16), and we all lost the full message in our separate camps and seminaries, which has lasted to our own time when there are some hopeful movements to recover it, such as the II Vatican Council and "emerging church" movement, and the recovery of contemplation.

Because we lost an actual sense of participation or any real transformation and de facto union with the divine, we largely lost any notion of the True Self too, which is who you objectively are, "hidden with

Christ in God, and when he is revealed—and he is your life—you too will be revealed in all your glory with him" (Colossians 3:3). It is all right there in that one quotation. What most of Christian history did was largely dress up and disguise the Christian False Self. We baptized it, confirmed it, married it, and made Christians go to church instead of realizing *they were* the church (1 Corinthians 3:17). We often gave "holy communion" to a self that was largely incapable of much communion, and even ordained as priest, minister, bishop, and pope many False Selves who did not even know, and much less know how to enjoy, their True Selves in God. This deserves immense sadness and grief, not hatred or disdain, and I hope I am coming across in a constructive way. Nothing less will help.

Those who have not come to the mystical banquet are not usually bad people or people rejected by God; they are just little people like you and me. Fortunately our very big God loves little people, maybe even preferentially (says the history of Israel itself, Job, Zephaniah, 1 Corinthians 12:22–23, Mary's Magnificat, and Jesus himself). *God loves his image in us forever*, according to the mystics. God cannot *not* love Christ in us, and we are only gradually "turned into the image that we reflect" (2 Corinthians 3:18). God's love was never withheld from us. But we were not always that capable of loving back or deeply loving ourselves or one another. That was, and continues to be, the problem.

Our True Self remains untouched for most of us, because any direct experience of God or explicit union with God was blocked, denied, and largely declared impossible. It always had to be mediated by a Bible, priest, minister, church, or sacrament, and very often the mediators, and the defending of their mediations, became the primary message itself. Most sermons reminded us quickly of our unworthiness before first telling us of our inherent worthiness. Many were then so deep in a black hole of low self-image that they had no way to climb back out. There was no foundation to build on, and all they could see was their weakness and incapacity. We have had no solid or objective foundation on which to build human personhood, and everybody was sent on their own—in total free fall. It did not need to be this way.

As many of the prophets said of Israel, there would always be a "remnant" who would hold onto the core message (Isaiah 4:3). They would be the yeast that would eventually leaven the whole dough, and Jesus built on this same lovely metaphor (Matthew 13:33). God has become accustomed to keeping the divine side of the covenant unilaterally—and always taking the initiative in that regard. As Paul puts it, "Can our lack of fidelity cancel God's fidelity? That would be absurd. God will always be true [Self], even though everyone is false [self]" (Romans 3:3–4).

God has always loved himself in us, even when we refuse to love and honor ourselves—just as any parent does with their self-destructive child. In some wonderful and imaginative ways, parents usually love the self-destructive child even more, and more patiently. "I have loved them as much as you loved me," Jesus says (John 17:23), which is a Trinitarian and absolute love. This is an ever-widening ripple of participation until it reaches the furthest edges of the human—and surely beyond the human to all of creation.

CHAPTER 6

If It Is True, It Is True Everywhere

There is one Body, one Spirit, "one and the same hope," there is one Lord, one faith, one initiation, and one God who is Father of all, over all, through all, and within all.

EPHESIANS 4:4–6

Christ likes us to prefer truth to himself, because before being Christ, he is truth. If one turns aside from him to go toward the truth, one will not go far before falling into his arms.

SIMONE WEIL, WAITING FOR GOD

Jews or Christians, or those of any other religion, should not feel that they were the first people who could know God's eternal patterns and presence. After all, those patterns are "perfectly plain since God has made it plain. Ever since God created the world, his everlasting power and deity—however invisible—have been there for the mind to see in the things that God has made" (Romans 1:19–20). How could any God worthy of the name be limited, stingy, or entirely invisible, or need to squeeze that which is Being itself into any specific time frame, culture, or vocabulary? If it is true, then all people of goodwill will be able to see it. That is what we mean by "the Perennial Tradition" that keeps recurring in new formulations.

As St. Bonaventure (1217–1274) put it, "[God] is an intelligible space whose center is everywhere and whose circumference is nowhere.... [God] is within all things, but not enclosed, outside all things but not excluded, above all things but not aloof, below all things but not debased.... [God] is supremely one and all-inclusive, [God] is therefore 'all in all'" (1 Corinthians 15:28).[1] You can either accuse St. Paul and St. Bonaventure, who is proclaimed a "Doctor of the Church," of pantheism, or admit that *we* are the ones who do not get it yet.

Jesus did say that we should "give the good news to all creation" (Mark 16:16). I can only assume that meant to enter into their worlds, learn their vocabulary, and humbly understand their assumptions, and not sit around and wait until they understand and totally agree with ours. Failure to even care to communicate to others makes any group a closed system, and not finally good news for anybody inside or outside. Note how Paul adjusts his words and ideas to each audience, which he even praises himself for (1 Corinthians 9:19–23). He says to the people of Athens (Acts 17:26–28), "All nations can seek the divine, can feel their way toward him, and succeed in finding him. He is not far from any of us, since *it is in him that we live, and move, and have our being* [emphasis mine]" (Acts 17:27–28). He then quotes several pagan sources to the effect that "we are all his children." He began this famous talk by admitting that we can "worship the God that I proclaim without even knowing it" (17:23). You apparently do not need to know you are worshiping God to be worshiping God. One really wonders how such texts were forgotten or ignored in the name of later closed house thinking. If Paul had not reached out to outsiders and made sense to "the Gentiles" and pagans, Christianity would have remained a small sect of Judaism, and most of us would not be reading this book today.

Perhaps God and consciousness and Being are the same thing. This ever-flowing abundance that we call God clearly loves and revels in endless manifestation, fecundity, and diversity. The Formless One is forever seeking new and fantastic forms. Just watch the Nature Channel, particularly shows on the deep seas or the insect world, which have been largely hidden to us up to now. There is surely no indication of any divine interest in blandness, uniformity, exclusion, mindless repetition, or sameness.

God is very clearly not a mere tribal God, and one would think the three monotheistic religions would have understood that message first and best. No group will ever confine or control God (see John 3:6–8, 4:23–24) to any little tent or temple, which has been the temptation since Exodus, yet every religion falls into it. How could anyone imagine God being small and still call this phenomenon God? Only with eyes wide shut. History, the shrinking globe, and Jesus' proclamation of the Kingdom of God are demanding of us a very big tent and a universal temple. It is God's one world, and if the supposed God lovers cannot see this, one wonders if there is any hope for this planet.

Thomas Aquinas, Bonaventure, and John Duns Scotus taught the same thing clearly and unequivocally: "*Deus est Ens*," that is, God is Being itself (which is different from saying that God is *a* Being or *all* Beings). Being did not just start showing itself with the Hindu scriptures, the Koran, or the Judeo-Christian era. If that were the case, God would have been silent, bored, and twiddling God's divine thumbs for a very long time indeed. Surely God was not just waiting for Orthodox Jews, Roman Catholics, and American evangelicals to show up, which is in the last nanosecond of known time.

In early Christianity, the search for the big pattern was called the "Vincentian canon" after St. Vincent of Lerin, who in 434 A.D. gave us the first known definition of the word *catholic*. In his classic Patristic text, he says that this is the way we could discern the truth from heresy: "Now in the catholic church itself we take the greatest care to hold *that which has been believed everywhere, always, and by all* [emphasis mine]. This alone is truly and properly 'catholic,' as is shown by the very force and meaning of the word, which means universality. We must hold to this rule if we are to be universal and ecumenical people."[2] It surely seems this canon should have been taught in all seminaries Orthodox, Roman, and Protestant, and that this is what we mean when we say the words of the Nicene Creed: "I believe in the one, holy, *catholic*, and apostolic church." Yet, most denominational seminaries have never heard of this very early Vincentian canon, which reveals our across-the-board bias toward tribal thinking. I would call his wisdom a central piece of the Perennial philosophy.

If it is truth, it has to be true everywhere or it is not true at all, St. Vincent is rightly saying. Such broad, deep, and mystical seeing must not be constricted into denominational "churchiness" or theological wrangling. If it is true, then science, psychology, poetry, and philosophy will also be seeing the same thing, but from different angles, at different levels, and with different vocabularies. We can still use the Vincentian canon and look for truth that is somehow held *"everywhere, always, and by all."* Perhaps no other generation has been more prepared to do just that than ours—and with solid scholarship and science at our disposal besides.

Right now, this still expanding universe would indicate that the first incarnation of God that we are aware of began at least 14.6 billion years ago, give or take a few years, when God first decided to "manifest and materialize." We now call that "the big bang." The *human incarnation*, however, took place two thousand years ago with the epiphany of Jesus, according to Christian belief. Jesus emerged from rich Jewish roots, the people who already recognized the I-Thou relationship between God and themselves.

"The Face of the Other" was only gradually showing itself in face-to-face form, so we could know how to relate personally to this awesome and boundless Mystery that is beyond conceptualization (1 John 1:1–4). For Christians, the Mystery is revealed forthrightly in the loving face of Jesus (John 1:18; 2 Corinthians 4:6). What an awesome leap of faith to believe this, as my Jewish and secular friends have often reminded me.

Cosmology is now offering a wonderful, and I do mean wonder-full, reimagining for much of theology. The truth is first of all written in creation itself—our first and primary Bible (Romans 1:19–20). And all of creation is saying from the beginning that things live, and things die, and things live again in new shapes. Christians say, "Christ dies, Christ lives, and Christ comes again," and call it "*the* mystery of faith." Buddhists point out the same pattern: "Emptiness is form and form is emptiness." We are both saying the same thing, but with different metaphors—ours is just personal, and theirs is more abstract and philosophical. *We are both saying that all things die and change forms, and nothing is permanent in its present state.* And now science is saying it too.

As a Christian however, I am not talking about reincarnation or resuscitation, but resurrection as such, which is quite different. Resurrection is not just changing forms but somehow an even improved or advanced form. Christians were the most prepared to believe in evolution, and then we ended up being the ones who fought it the most. I think this reveals how little we reflected on the actual Gospel accounts (see Appendix B).

Furthermore, Jesus' words to the Sadducees, who did not believe in resurrection, take on a whole new significance in this discussion. He says to them, "God is not a God of the dead, but of the living. For to him, *all humans are in fact alive*" (Luke 20:38). I think we need to chew on that for a while and not too quickly return to our predigested Christian response. In the authentic search for God, the field keeps expanding and never tightening. As in the universe itself, we move toward an ever greater aliveness, a greater consciousness, a deeper union. Pierre Teilhard de Chardin called this *a divine allurement*, which is calling the universe forward until a truly cosmic "Christ comes to full stature" (Ephesians 4:13). For him, this was the *Omega Point* of all history which made the universe unified, meaningful, and hopeful. There is a trajectory and direction to it all, which is what both Jews and Christians were supposed to believe. But few people will put together science, philosophy, mysticism, and poetry as brilliantly as does this French Jesuit.[3]

For any Christians who are alarmed as they read here, such integration does not make the Judeo-Christian message less true, but actually much larger and even more compelling, unless you prefer to be tribal instead of "catholic" in the original Vincentian sense. Do you want the Gospel to be small truth or Great Truth? This is the question that many Christians must ask themselves.

Science is no longer our enemy; instead quantum physics, biology, and other academic disciplines are revealing science as probably our new and best partner, much better than philosophy ever was. If something is spiritually true, it will also be true in the physical world too, and all religions will somehow be looking at that "one truth" from different angles, goals, assumptions, and vocabulary, as will all of the disciplines of any great university. If we are really convinced that we have the Great Big Truth, then we should also be able to trust that others will see it from their different angles — or it is not a great big truth. No one wants to be our enemy unless they assume that we ourselves have chosen to live in our own small tent and cannot talk to them or do not want to talk to them on their terms. We are the ones who have too often assumed ill will and been far too eager to create enemies instead of realizing that others often enjoyed very similar "good news" but inside different packaging.

Big Truth is written in reality itself before it was ever written in books. If you say yes to Reality, "what is," you will recognize the same truth when it shows itself in any Bible. If you do not respond to the good, the true, and the beautiful in Reality, I doubt if you will ever see it in the best Bible translation in the world. If it is the truth, it is true all the time and everywhere, and sincere lovers of truth will take it wherever it comes from. If it is true, it is common domain, and "there for the mind to see in the things that God has made" (Romans 1:20). Or, as Aquinas was fond of saying, "If it true, it is always from the one Holy Spirit." The important question is not, "Who said it?" but, "Is it true?"

I do not believe the will of God is a theory, an argued moral theology, or an abstraction in any form; it is *seeking the truth of each situation in that situation as best as we can figure it out*. What else could God ask of humanity, most of whom had no access to synagogue, temple, church, Koran, moral theology class, or Bible? Were they all utterly lost and rejected? Somehow the True Self in all humans has a natural access to that "hidden" will of God—if the mind and heart and soul are open and undefended (which is always the spiritual task and not easily achieved).

Jeremiah called it "the law written in your heart" (31:33). The Catholic tradition called it "natural law" or "natural theology." The soul or True Self has responded naturally to the soul of other things since the beginning of human consciousness. The False Self almost always distorts even good things, because it still thinks "it's all about me"—and it never is.

Perhaps Moses said it poetically and best and very early on: "This law is not beyond your strength or beyond your reach. It is not in heaven, so that you need to wonder, 'Who will go up to heaven and bring it down to us so that we may hear it and keep it?' Nor is it beyond the seas, so that you need to wonder, 'Who will cross the seas for us so that we might hear it and keep it?' No, the Word is very near to you. It is in your mouth and in your heart" (Deuteronomy 30:11–14).

Jews call this Word the Law; Christians call it the *Logos* or the blueprint; Taoists call it the Eternal Tao; Buddhists call it Emptiness or the Great Compassion;

Hindus call it Brahman; Sufi Muslims call it the dance; and science speaks of universal theories. But we are all pointing to one underlying truth that we all strive toward in ten thousand ways. We all somehow believe it is a coherent and even a benevolent universe. Maybe that is the very heart of the meaning of faith. It is surely the Perennial Tradition discovered by all people of goodwill and sincere search.

Perhaps our cultural icon, Wendell Berry, is a good guide for us at this point. He often says that "the mind that is not baffled is not employed"! The major spiritual problem for many religious people is that they refuse to be baffled for a while.

CHAPTER 7

Enlightenment at Gunpoint

 Letting go is not a choice. None of the transformations of the dying process are a choice.... Imagine if you will, water rushing toward a drain.
KATHLEEN DOWLING SINGH

The flowing back will correspond to the flowing out.
MEISTER ECKHART, O.P.

It is no surprise that we humans would deny death's certain coming, fight it, and seek to avoid the demise of the only self we have ever known. As Kathleen Dowling Singh puts it in her groundbreaking book, *The Grace in Dying*, "It is the experience of 'no exit,' a recognition of the fact that the situation is inescapable, that one is utterly at the mercy of the power of the Ground of Being ... it is absurd and monstrous."[1]

"The Ground of Being," a commanding phrase that Paul Tillich used, is an excellent metaphor for what most of us would call God (Acts 17:28). For Singh, it is the source and goal that we both deeply desire and desperately fear. It is the *Mysterium Tremendum* of Rudolf Otto, which is both alluring and frightful at the same time. Both God and death feel like "engulfment," as when you first gave yourself totally to another person. It is the very union that will liberate us, yet we resist, retrench, and run. It is no surprise that historic male initiation rites forced the young man to face both God and death head-on—ahead of time—so he could know for himself that it could do his True Self no harm—but in fact would reveal it.[2]

The path of dying and rising is exactly what any in-depth spiritual teaching must aim for. It alone allows us to say afterward, "What did I ever lose by dying?" It is the letting go of all you think you are, moving into a world without any experienced context, and becoming the person you always were anyway—which you always knew at depth, and yet did not know at all on the surface. That must be the first great surprise of heaven and why I think our first word will likely be a great big YES! —with the clenched fist and elbow thrust to the ground that young men and women love to display in victory.

The final surrender of our False Self in the last months, weeks, days, and hours in any conscious dying might well be called "enlightenment at gunpoint," according to Singh. Not all people get to enjoy this luxury, although it should be sought after. We have made the inherently spiritual event of death into a mere medical event. Families were meant to accompany their loved ones across, and all the Sunday school or catechism classes in the world will never make up for this loss to spiritual consciousness. I would say exactly the same for birth.

We put off enlightenment by decades if we are not present at births and deaths. Remember that salvation is not so much a matter of *if*, as it is *when* you get it, and maybe also how much can you handle. "Don't be afraid, trust in God and trust in me. There are many rooms in my Father's house," Jesus says (John 14:1–2). When he said that the reign of God is "at hand" (Mark 1:15) or "in your midst" (Luke 17:21), my presumption is that he was saying this largely to Jews, Canaanites, "sinners," pagans, and other Christian "unworthies." He is announcing universal access to God.

Why, oh why, did we make the Gospel into a competition instead of a joyous proclamation of this necessary but good process — of surrender into love?

I think it is because the ego (the False Self) prefers win-lose over win-win, even strangely enough, when it ends up defining oneself as a loser. The ego will always choose trumped-up competition over any calm cooperation. We would sooner run a risky NASCAR race that only one, or a few, of us can win than allow God to win with everybody. It is almost the American way. Such a mind-set is of itself "hell." It is nothing more than spiritual capitalism. God's big win is accurately called heaven. Heaven is God's victory celebration, not ours! And the banner over the eternal banquet table will say one thing: "Love is stronger than death."

DEATH AND FEAR

I am aware of the phrase "true self" occurring only once in the Bible. Paul uses the words to describe what he is desperately trying to locate in the midst of some major trials with his False Self, and he speaks of it in a telling way: "When I act against my own will, then it is not my *true self* doing it, but sin which lives in me" (Romans 7:20). Somehow he knows there is a part of him that is objective, true, and unafraid of death. And then he contrasts that with what we are calling the False Self (7:14–25) and calls it "sin." This sin is our cozy image of ourselves as individual and autonomous. When "this body" is all you think you are, no wonder you are afraid of dying. It is all you know and have — if you have not discovered your soul, that is. The False Self is terrified of death, because it knows this mental ego that it calls "myself" will die, and it cannot find any long-term alternative to it, so it works for short term instead. The False Self has no substance, no permanence, no vitality, only various forms of immediate gratification.

Whenever you are fearing death, physical death or death of some ego fixation, or using diversionary tactics of any kind, you are in your False Self at that moment. Again, it is not usually bad or evil, but just inadequate to the big questions of love, death, suffering, God, or any notion of infinity. God allows and uses all our diversionary tactics to get us to the full destination. That is how perfect and patient divine love is. God probably knows we are procrastinators much more than perpetrators.

The True Self will surely have doubts about the unknown too. But as such, the True Self is not afraid of death. It has been there and back. The Risen Christ in you always knows that it will never lose anything real by dying, But you will not know that until you walk the whole gauntlet sincerely at least once. In my book *Falling Upward*, I called it "necessary suffering," that is, the necessary suffering of walking the full human path. That is what Jesus did and why we try to "reproduce the pattern of his death," each in our own way, so that we also can take our place in the "force field" of resurrection (Philippians 2:11–12). Often Paul needs physical words to describe these states, which I think is quite telling. Spirit and spirituality have a material component, and we all ride the embodied waves of both life and death. Who of us has not said, "I could cut the fear with a knife," or, "The joy was contagious and palpable"? For me, the Holy Spirit, resurrection, and evil are all very real and even physical "force fields."[3]

Once you know you are sharing in *the force field of resurrection*, you can always draw on it, live within it, and move out from it. The pressed clay or "dust" of Adam has then become the immortal diamond that is Christ. The breathing into Adam (Genesis 2:7) has become the breathing out of Jesus (John 20:22), and you are now sharing the breath of the one Spirit. The incarnation has become resurrection in you. "Church" in any form should be a "laboratory for resurrection," or the "conspiracy of God" as Father John Haughey beautifully called it years ago (*con-spirare* = to breathe with, or where we learn to breathe as one). And no one, or no group, will ever have control this breath-wind-spirit. "It blows where it wills," John says (3:8).

Nevertheless, the price of such momentous realization is that you must first "go into the tomb" with Jesus (Romans 6:4) or at least wait attentively at other people's tombs as the Marys did (Matthew 27:61). It is significant that all accounts have the women visiting or accompanying death, and they come out the other side much more quickly than the men do. You can learn the essentials by strong identification and accompaniment of others in their death walk. Solidarity with other people's suffering teaches as much as direct suffering does, and often more so because of love. Just ask good hospice workers, who are emerging as some of the wisest "practical theologians" around today. Visiting and caring for the sick and accompanying the dying and dead is their seminary. This kind of companionship has been called a "corporal work of mercy," but now we know that it is the visitors who often receive the wisdom more than those who are visited. Some call this "reverse theology" because it turns just about everything on its head.

C. G. Jung, often very critical of Christianity, said that the "Archetype of the God-Man" (Christ) is a relatively adequate map of the unconscious human journey, and it should not be dismissed until and unless one has walked through it oneself. He feared that Western civilization would lose this map and that it would be quite dangerous and disastrous for us if we let this map wither in our midst. In that sense, we need an effective "Savior" who can name and guide us on the necessary path. Without a good map, Jung feared the manipulation, violation, and even "annulment" of the human personality.[4] That sounds like an overstatement until you note the hugely destructive *isms* of our time: totalitarian communism, Nazism, consumerism itself, materialism in general, and what John Paul II called "rigid capitalism," all of which deny many of the essentials of humanness, and often our very core.

The risen Jesus is not being rewarded for a job well done as much as he is mirroring the full completed journey and goal. He is the "pioneer and perfecter" of the entire journey, as Hebrews (12:2) poetically puts it. He comes out the other side shouting, as it were, "See it is true, love is indeed stronger than death! If you ever doubt it, just look at me." He is the "guarantee" (7:22), the "pledge and promise" (Ephesians 1:14), *that love works*. So that we would not forget, that guarantee has been implanted in each human heart and keeps quietly ticking away. Some spiritual directors wisely call it "your deepest level of desiring." The Holy Spirit is God desiring in you and through you—until it becomes your desiring too.

Even the human mind of Jesus did not know some things until he came out the other side of death. In fact, I do not believe the human mind of Jesus fully knew his own True Self as the "Son of God" until after the Resurrection. Before his own transformation, Jesus lived in faith and "was like us in all ways except sin" (Hebrews 4:15). Jesus never appeared to believe the "lie of separation," which is the core meaning of sin. He said without hesitation, "I and the Father are one" (John 10:30). That made him indeed unique—and the ultimate model and leader for all of humanity.

All of us have to walk the human journey, some way, some day—from the Neanderthals to those walking on Madison Avenue today. All either have died or will soon die. It is only the exact circumstances that change, but it is the same "One God who is Father of all, over all, through all and within all" (Ephesians 4:6) who is *taking all of this dying home*. If not, the

vast number of very short lives — young soldiers who
die in battle, women in childbirth, Natives with small-
pox, children who starve to death, and the suffering
of disabled bodies and tortured prisoners — make this
world a major Greek tragedy that is almost impossible to imagine as any kind of victory for God or for
anybody else.

*The Crucified One is God's standing solidarity with
the suffering, the tragedy, and the disaster of all time,
and God's promise that it will not have the final word.*

*The Risen One is God's final word about the uni-
verse and what God plans to do with all suffering.*

ABOUT DYING

In all of nature, one form has to die and decay
for another to take over, so this pattern should be
obvious and clear, although it is largely not — until you
really observe or actually study the patterns of almost
everything.[5] Again, we appear to be in gross denial.

Jesus' own dying has to be made quite clear and
forthright in the Gospels; in Mark, it is almost half of
the text. His "necessary death" had to be made visible
and compelling because we all want to deny death and
avoid the obvious. Quite unfortunately, we made

Jesus' necessary dying into a mechanical atonement theory demanded by a "just" God, which had the side effect of keeping the spotlight away from our own necessary dying. Jesus indeed became our scapegoat, but not at all in the way that he intended. Avoiding our own necessary "pattern of dying" (Philippians 3:11), we constructed instead a kind of metaphysical transaction, called "paying the price" or "opening the gates," that was necessary for Jesus to complete. Then we worshiped him for doing this, which is understandable, but *also avoids the point that we all have to pay the price* for growing up and for loving.

Jesus never said, "Worship me," but he often said, "Follow me." We have wasted a lot of good energy on "vicarious substitutionary atonement theories" and created a punitive and petty God in the process — a "Father God" who was incapable of forgiving "without blood."[6] Is God that unfree? Remember, the ego likes contests of win and lose and cannot even comprehend anything like win-win. Jesus became our substitute in losing, hoping it would let us off the hook, I guess.

Fortunately, we Franciscans never officially believed this common substitutionary atonement theory. We were always a kind of *alternative orthodoxy* inside Catholicism. In the teaching of John Duns Scotus,

Jesus was pure gracious gift, and not necessary at all (John 1:16; Ephesians 1:3–6). God operated out of total and absolute freedom in the gift of Jesus and the Christ to the world.[7] Incarnation, the birth in Bethlehem, was already God's unconditional choice and gift of himself to us. Incarnation was already redemption. And why would a free gift be less beautiful than a necessity? Why would an act of violence be necessary to redeem the world? For us, *Jesus did not come to change the mind of God about humanity but to change the mind of humanity about God. It is "simple and beautiful;" as Einstein said great truth would always have to be.*

This teaching alone made me glad I joined the Franciscans. Jesus' death was not solving any cosmic problem whatsoever, but revealing to us our own human problem: that *we fear, and we kill what we should love.* And what do we fear most of all? That death is stronger than love. Jesus in his Cross and Resurrection uncovered and undid both of these lies forever. That is what we are singing about at Easter with all those happy songs about overcoming death. The big pattern leading to transformation or Resurrection says that there is a gate that you must pass through, even though the gate has a thousand forms: *you must die before you die—and then you will know how to die and not be afraid of it.* The Risen Presence always appears once your False Self stops attaching, defending, denying, and blaming. As in Matthew's account (28:9), he just walks up and says, "Hi!"

Paul actually says in several places that "our former selves have been crucified" already (Romans 6:6). The False Self is fragile and temporary and is thus already "over and out." Its death knell has already rung. It is just a matter of time until you touch the true, and the false falls away like clumsy scaffolding. This is probably why some saints were pictured holding or looking at a human skull. It was not meant to be morbid but a way of picturing this shock of realization and the utter change of consciousness that follows.

Once you experience the Real, the unreal is increasingly a mere diversion or entertainment, not substantial reality. Once you encounter the Risen Presence, you can rather easily let go of the past and the petty. The Risen Christ could be called the "future shock" of God. The Gospel accounts make note that the Resurrection occurs "very early on the first day of the week" (John 20:1), clearly evoking a new creation, a fresh start, a new first (Genesis 1:3–5), but now an eternal day of Easter light. And, of course, scientists now tell us that all light in the universe is electromagnetically connected and that all natural light is in fact *one*. The Risen Christ is the personification of this one Light that includes all light, which is why he is always described as "dazzling white" or "like lightning" (Matthew 28:3).

ATTACHMENT AND DETACHMENT

The very quality of what we call life is that when we are in touch with our True Self, our existence reveals itself as somehow eternal, gratuitous, endlessly outflowing, and inherently trustworthy (Romans 8:35–39). Such life cannot die. True life is eternal because it includes everything. Life, like water, is inherently resourceful and flows into whatever channel allows it. True life always morphs into love, forgives everything for being that thing, and thus is much stronger than death (Song of Songs 8:6). That is the real and lasting meaning of the resurrection of the Christ, and it far surpasses any arguments for or against a mere bodily resurrection.

Remember, please remember, you do not (you must not!) fear, attack, or hate the False Self. That would only continue a negative and arrogant death energy, and it is delusional and counterproductive anyway. It would be trying to "drive out the devil by the prince of devils," as Jesus puts it. In the great economy of grace, all is used and transformed, and nothing is wasted. God uses your various False Selves to lead you beyond them. Note that Jesus' clear message to his beloved, Mary Magdalene, is not that she squelch, deny, or destroy her human love for him. He is much more subtle than that. He just says to her, "Do not cling to me" (John 20:17). He is saying, "Don't hold on to your needy False Self. We are all heading for something much bigger and much better, Mary." This is the spiritual art of detachment, which is not taught much in capitalistic worldview where clinging and possessing are not just the norm but even the goal. You see how trapped we are.

Great love is both very attached ("passionate") and yet very detached at the same time. It is love but not addiction. The soul, the True Self, has everything, and so it does not require any particular thing. When you have all things, you do not have to protect any one thing. True Self can love and let go. The False Self cannot do this. The "do not cling to me" encounter between Jesus and Mary Magdalene is the most painted Easter scene, I am told. The artistic imagination knew that a seeming contradiction was playing out here:

intense love and yet appropriate distance. The soul and the spirit tend to love and revel in paradoxes; they operate by resonance and reflection. The ego (False Self) wants to resolve all paradoxes in a most glib way and thinks that it can. It operates in a way that is mechanical and instrumental. This is not always bad, but it is surely limited.

The ego would like Mary Magdalene and Jesus to be caught up in a passionate love affair. Of course they are, in the deepest sense of the term, but only the True Self knows how to enjoy and picture "a love of already satisfied desire." The True Self and False Self see differently; both are necessary, but one is better, bigger, and even eternal.

GOD AND DEATH

There is no hatred or violence in God. The absolute allowings of all history should make it rather clear that God cannot be violent, or punitive, or even in control. The Divine One did not stop the torturing of the Inquisition or the gas chambers of the Holocaust. God somehow uses death, and our own mistakes, even evil itself, to bring us all to full life. But God does not punish us with catastrophes or even stop catastrophes.

"Neither he nor his parents sinned," Jesus said, "he was born blind that the works of God might be displayed in him" (John 9:3). God's total commitment to love becomes a total commitment to freedom, which means God had to give up all enforcement and control. God is clearly not a policeman. This is a huge price for God and us to pay, which might well be revealed in the broken body of Jesus itself.[8] But there is no other way for God to act, for God is love itself (1 John 4:8, 16), which seems to be the only kind of power God uses now, after the original omnipotence of creation itself.

By now, you might have realized that *our fear of death is actually our fear of God. If we resolve one, we normally resolve the other*. To totally resolve the God issue would be to totally resolve the death issue. And we have the full wherewithal to do just that! That wherewithal we call Trinity, which is saying that God is an outpouring in one direction. God is only for and never against. Let me try to explain (as if you could explain the Trinity!).

The notion of God as Trinity is the foundation of all Christian thought, and yet it never has been! Our dualistic minds sort of shelved the whole thing out of embarrassment. No good Christian would deny it, but as Karl Rahner said, "Should the doctrine of the Trinity have to be dropped as false, the major part of religious literature could well remain virtually unchanged."[9] Many still fear that a trinitarian notion of God is too Christian, a mathematical conundrum, a harmless "shamrock," or somehow contradictory to monotheism, whereas good trinitarian theology often has the exact opposite effect in practical interfaith dialogue.

First, it says that God is more a verb than a noun: God is three "relations," which of itself is mind-boggling for most believers. Yet it opens up an honest notion of God as Mystery who can never be fully understood with our rational, instrumental, mechanical minds. God is a process rather than a clear name or idea, a communion, Interbeing itself, and never an isolated deity that can be captured by our mind.

Christians believe that God is formlessness (the Father), God is form (the Son), and God is the very life and love energy between those two (the Holy Spirit). The three do not cancel one another out; rather, they do exactly the opposite. God is relationship itself and known in relationship, which opens up a huge conversation with the world of science and physics and therapy too. What a wonderful surprise this is, yet it names everything correctly at the core — from atoms, to ecosystems, to families, to galaxies. The doctrine of the Trinity was made to order to defeat the dualistic mind and invite us into nondual, holistic consciousness. It replaced the argumentative principle of two with the dynamic principle of three. It leaves us inside the wonderfully open space of "not one, but not two either." *Sit stunned* with that for a few minutes.

The main point I want to make here, hoping that the more inquisitive among you will now read further,[10] is that the most ancient and solid theology of the Trinity proceeding from the Cappadocian fathers of the third and fourth centuries, and adopted by the Councils of the Church, says that God is a circle dance (*perichoresis*) of total outpouring and perfect receiving among three intimate partners, who receive their Total Self from another and then hand it on to another, who repeats the self-emptying act of love to a third.

As Catherine LaCugna says at the end of *God for Us*, her monumental study of the history of the doctrine of the Trinity, if this is true, then any notion of God not giving, not outpouring, not surrendering itself, not totally loving is *a theological impossibility and absurdity. God only and always loves.*[11] You cannot reverse, slow down, or limit an overflowing waterwheel of divine compassion and mercy. It goes in only one, constant, and eternal, direction—toward ever more life and ever more creative life, and a love that is stronger than death. All personhood is received personhood, and never self-generated.

The world of science, biology, and astrophysics is now affirming this trinitarian truth from very different angles. These disciplines see that all of creation is relationship. All is a constant changing of forms through a nonstop process of loss and renewal, death and resurrection, losing the self and finding a larger self—just as in God and in the teaching of Jesus. I hope this allows us to trust death, to trust God, and even to trust ourselves a bit more now. Even the two-steps-backward moments are for the sake of three steps forward.

The backsplashes from any waterwheel do not keep the waterwheel of life from flowing in its one generous and constant direction. That is exactly why we can say that you do not need to be afraid of death and you do not need to be afraid of God.

CHAPTER 8

Intimate with Everything

> *Love all God's creation, the whole and every grain of sand in it. Love every leaf, every ray of God's light. Love the animals, love the plants, love everything. If you love everything, you will perceive the divine mystery in things. Once you perceive it, you will begin to understand it better every day. And you will come at last to love the whole world with an all-embracing love.... Things flow and are indirectly linked together, and if you push here, something will move at the other end of the world. If you strike here, something somewhere will wince; if you sin here, something somewhere will suffer.*
>
> FYODOR DOSTOYEVSKY, THE BROTHERS KARAMAZOV

Intimacy could be described as our capacity for closeness and tenderness toward things. It is often revealed in moments of risky self-disclosure. Intimacy lets itself out and lets the other in. It makes all love possible, and yet it also reveals your utter incapacity to love back as the other deserves. Intimacy therefore encompasses a loneliness, but a sweet loneliness. In intimate moments, *you have been touched by something you cannot yet endure or carry, but you still love the touch and the invitation to carry*. You are always larger after any intimate encounter; in fact, it might well be the only way to enlarge spiritually. It is always grace.

As I studied accounts of the Resurrection, I came to see what is now completely obvious to me: these texts reveal both the Christ and the True Self as a deep capacity for intimacy with yourself and with everything, probably including life itself. Starting with Christ's "white as snow" robe and his "face like lightning" (Matthew 28:3), we have initial statements of perfect transparency, accessibility, and radiant visibility. The True Self is a shared and sharable self, or it is not the True Self.

But there is more. The Risen Christ comes to meet others and does not demand that they search for him (Matthew 28:9, 16, 18). Surely "I am with you always" (28:20) is the way that lovers describe their faithfulness while dating or at their wedding. Jesus first appears to his female friend, Mary Magdalene, and not to his mother, which has always been a bit problematic. It was offensive to Catholics because they thought "the Virgin Mary" should surely come first, to the sexually suspicious for obvious reasons, and to Jews because a Jewish mother would surely expect it. Nevertheless, the phrase commonly used throughout is that "he showed himself" (Mark 16:12, John 21:1), which is the language of intimates. In Luke's account, he joins in an easy walk with two ordinary travelers, invites them to tell their story of heartbreak, and accepts their invitation to stay with them; when he leaves them, it is with "burning hearts." He explains to them his own life narrative — he "opens up," as we say — and, sure enough, "their eyes were opened up" too (Luke 24:31–32).

To the scared-stiff disciples, a "flesh and blood" presence "appears" in the midst of their "alarm and fright" (Luke 24:37–39) and offers himself both body and soul: "It is I indeed. Touch me and see for yourself" (24:39), and he shows them his wounded hands and feet. They are "dumbfounded with joy" (24:41). It is the speechlessness and wonder of union regained, like a lover's sustained grin after a painful estrangement.

In all accounts, the Risen Body still carries Christ's scars and reveals them too — hands, feet, and side are all mentioned. Remember that resurrection is not woundedness denied, forgotten, or even totally healed. It is always *woundedness transformed*. You still carry your scars forever, as both message and trophy. They still "hurt" in a way, which keeps you mindful and humble, but they no longer allow you to hurt other people. Pain transformed is no longer pain transmitted.

In John's account, we have "the disciple Jesus loved" getting to the encounter and believing more quickly than the boss, Peter. The fact that the text bothers to describe this race to the tomb is significant, seemingly saying that love will get you to resurrection more quickly than power, office, or role (John 20:3–10). Here Mary Magdalene knows Jesus not by sight but when he pronounces her first name (20:16). She completes the exchange by calling him "Master" in return. Jesus' puzzling "Do not cling to me" (20:17) statement is what makes true intimacy possible. Intimacy is possible only between two calm identities and is not the same as melding or fusing into one. As we say in nondual teaching, "Not two but not one either."

Jesus' passing through closed doors twice (John 20:19, 26) is an obvious statement of the risk and price of self-disclosure, especially as it mentions each time that he exposed his hands and his side to them. To Thomas he daringly says, "Put your finger here.... Give me your hand, and put it into my side" (20:27), an uncommon exchange of male intimacy that brings forth an ecstatic response of trust and adoration.

And finally, Jesus invites Peter to respond three times to what well might have been an unmanly, although surely vulnerable, question: "Do you love me?" (John 21:15–17). Fortunately, Peter does not just reply, "I love you too," but says, "You *know* that I love you." That is what intimates want from one another — not just that they are in union, but that the other knows and enjoys this union as much as they do. Surely we all have experienced that rush of excitement, and it is precisely in this knowledge that the mutual joy of lovers and close friends consists.

The inner knowledge of God's love is itself the Indwelling Presence, and it is also described as joy (John 15:11). Peter will soon realize that his threefold denial on the night Jesus was taken away has been graciously undone and erased by three opportunities to name his love, and without even mentioning his denials. This lovely exchange between Jesus and Peter teaches clearly how God deals with the soul, the True Self. This is how any true friend protects and creates the other. And how could divine love ever be less than the most loving friend you ever had?

But which comes first? Does feeling safe and held by God allow you to deal with others in the same way? Or does human tenderness allow you to imagine that God must be the same, but infinitely so? I do not suppose it really matters where you start; the important thing is that you get in on the big secret from one side or the other.

Yes, "secret," or even "hidden secret," is what people like the Psalmist (25:14), Paul, Rumi, Hafiz, Bonaventure, Lady Julian, and many mystics called it. And for some sad reason, it seems to be a well-kept secret. Jesus praises God for "hiding these things from the learned and the clever and revealing them only to the little ones" (Matthew 11:25). Well, what is it that the learned and the clever often cannot see? And why do only "little ones" see it?

The big and hidden secret is this: an infinite God seeks and desires intimacy with the human soul. Once you experience such intimacy, only the intimate language of lovers describes what is going on for you: mystery, tenderness, singularity, specialness, changing the rules "for me," nakedness, risk, ecstasy, incessant longing, and, of course also, suffering. This is the mystical vocabulary of the saints.

One's biggest secrets and deepest desires are usually revealed to others, and even discovered by ourselves, in the presence of sorrow, failure, or need—when we are very vulnerable and when one feels entirely safe in the arms of someone's love. That is why all "little ones" have a huge head start. When vulnerable exchange happens, there is always a broadening of being on both sides. We are bigger and better people afterward. Those who never go there always remain small and superficial and unconnected to themselves. You would normally experience it as a lack of substance or even reality in a person. People who have avoided all intimacy normally do not know who they are at any depth—and cannot tell others who *they* are. This is the real "evil" of mere promiscuous sex.

Only when we are in such a tender place can God safely reveal the "inside" of God to us. All self-sufficient ones remain outsiders to the mystery of divine love because they will always misuse it. They have actually blocked its possibility and stopped its give-and-take by their hardness. Many of the mystics speak of God "hiding" *himself or herself* now and then. (Even any notion of gender is smaller than God.) I believe this is the way love has to work: you can give more only when you see how the other used and enjoyed a first dose of love. Has it opened the channel or closed it? Divine love continues to be poured out forever as long as we are not "misusing" it or keeping it to ourselves. If you try to misuse infinite love, it "hides," and you cannot go deeper. This is why many remain at the level of mere "religion," and it is surely what Jesus means when he says "to those who have, more will be given and they will have more than enough; and to those who have not, they will lose even what they do have" (Matthew 13:12). This is not spiritual capitalism; it is just the way love works.

Only the need of a beloved knows how to receive the need and gift of the lover, and only the need of a lover knows how to receive the need and gift of the beloved without misusing such love. A mutually admitted emptiness is the ultimate safety net for all love, and in the Scriptures, even God is presented as somehow "needing" us and even "jealous" for our love (Exodus 20:5, 34:14). Basically love works only inside humility. My father, St. Francis, fell in love with the humility of God, a word that most of us would not even think could apply to God.[1]

Fullness in a person cannot permit love because there are no openings, no handles, no give-and-take, and no deep hunger. It is like trying to attach two inflated balloons to one another. Human vulnerability gives the soul an immense head start on its travels — maybe the only start for any true spiritual journey. Thus, the Risen Christ starts us off by revealing *the human wounds of God*, God's total solidarity with human suffering. He starts with self-disclosure from the divine side, which ideally leads to self-disclosure from our side. The Bible first opened up for me in the 1960s when the II Vatican Council said that divine revelation was not God disclosing ideas about God but actually God disclosing "himself" [*sic*].[2] Quickly Scripture, and religion itself, became not mere doctrines or moralisms for me, but love-making, an actual mutual exchange of being and intimacy.

The mystics, and those like Moses (Exodus 33:12–23), Jesus (John 5:19–20), and John the Divine (1 John 1:1–3) who personally claim to know God, are always aware that they have been let in on a big and wondrous love secret. Anyone not privy to an inner dialogue, that is, some kind of I-Thou relationship, would call such people presumptuous, emotional, foolish, or even arrogant. How could they presume to claim an actual union with the divine? But this is without doubt "God's secret, in which all the jewels of wisdom and knowledge are hidden" (Colossians 2:3). The insiders know that "anyone who loves is born of God and knows God. Anyone who fails to love can never know God, because God is love" (1 John 4:8). Such an amazing, but seldom quoted line, lets you in on the big secret and also makes it universal and available to all.

So how do you communicate to others what is inherently a secret? Or can you? How can the secret become "unhidden"? It becomes unhidden when people stop hiding—from God, themselves, and at least one other person. The emergence of our True Self is actually the big disclosure of the secret. Such risky self-disclosure is what I mean by intimacy, and intimacy is the way that love is transmitted. Some say the word comes from the Latin *intimus*, referring to that which is interior or inside. Some say its older meaning is found by *in timor*, or "into fear." In either case, the point is clear: intimacy happens when we reveal and expose our insides, and this is always scary. One never knows if the other can receive what is exposed, will respect it, or will run fast in the other direction. One must be prepared to be rejected. It is always a risk. The pain of rejection after self-disclosure is so great that it often takes a lifetime for people to risk it again.

Because I am ordained and older and have a public reputation, it is very easy for many people to put me on an utterly false pedestal. Many significant breakthroughs in spiritual direction or counseling work have occurred, however, when I mirrored for the confidant my own struggles, failures, sin, neediness, and weaknesses. There are plenty to go around, I assure you. But only then can the transmission happen. Once they know I am not above and beyond them, but exist in trial and error just as they do, the floodgates invariably open. If Richard is not at all perfect, they seem to think, then I can safely share my deeper secrets too.

Our fear of inferiority and the harsh judgments of others seals everything inside us. This is surely our False Self taking control because it fears all loss of control. And how did I learn such a pattern of mirroring and disclosure? Because many people have done the same for me. Even Jesus has revealed his "sacred heart" to me.[3] Spiritual wisdom is passed on from person to person, which is the real and lasting meaning of "apostolic succession." You can give away as a gift only what you have yourself received as a gift.

God takes this risk every moment of our existence, and most of us run from such an impossible divine seduction: "See, I have branded you on the palms of my hand," Yahweh says to Israel (Isaiah 49:16). As Paul puts it, we are sons (and daughters) and heirs, and not slaves or servant (Galatians 4:7). How, we ask, could God, "who is so rich—become so poor for our sake, [except] to make us rich out of his poverty" (2 Corinthians 8:9)? And that is exactly what the moment of intimacy always is, even from God. It is always a moment of "poverty" from one side or the other—or both. It is this opening that we all wait and long for. Then one side calls forth and also creates the other—and neither side needs or wants to take the credit. I hope you have been there, or there is something essential you do not know. It is the essence of what we mean by grace, the ecstasy of intimacy.

We need and belong to one another, love says—we are not our own. That is why St. Francis loved the very word *poverty* (*poverta*) and saw humility and vulnerability as the shocking, impossible nature of God, as revealed to him in Jesus (Philippians 2:6–8). *Poverty* is probably the Franciscan word for intimacy, which is why Francis even wanted to "marry Lady Poverty." Jesus tellingly begins his Sermon on the Mount with praise for the "poor in spirit" (Matthew 5:3). God could only tell us to be what God also is. It was the humility and poverty of God that Francis fell in love with—and married. A False Self could not bear the stripped-down poverty of this intangible intimacy with God. If there were no other evidence in his life, this willingness and desire to love a "poor" God would reveal how fully Francis of Assisi lived from his True Self.

It is almost impossible to fall in love with majesty, power, or perfection. These make us both fearful and codependent, but seldom truly loving. On some level, love can happen only between equals, and vulnerability levels the playing field. What Christians believe is that God somehow became our equal when he became the human "Jesus," a name that is, without doubt, the vulnerable name for God.

True human or divine intimacy is somewhat rare and very hard for all of us, but particularly for us men and for all who deem themselves to be *important people*, that is, those who are trained to protect their boundaries, to take the offensive, and to be afraid of all weakness or neediness. God begins thawing this glacial barrier by coming precisely in male form as Jesus, who then exposes maleness itself as naked, needy, and nailed to a tree. Most cultures would say that is mind blowing, heart exploding, and surely impossible. Only those who have been there on some cross of their own would continue to gaze on such an embarrassment and not turn away in discomfort (Zechariah 12:10). Thus, the transmission of the secret, the inner mystery of God, continues in space and time primarily through what Jesus calls again and again "the little ones" and "the poor in spirit," which he himself became.

Let me end by referring to a recent blog I wrote; I was amazed at the quality and quantity of the responses.[4] When this kind of response happens, you know you are hitting on "the real" for people. Here, in paraphrase, is part of what I wrote: I think that many of us men, celibate men even more, are very afraid of intimacy. I am going to make a rather absolute statement: people who risk intimacy are invariably happier and much more real people. They feel like they have lots of "handles" that allow others to hold on to them and that allow them to hold onto themselves. People who avoid intimacy are always, and I mean always, imprisoned in a small and circular world. *Intimacy is the only gateway into the temple of human or divine love.*[5]

One good thing about celibacy is that it can tell us that an awful lot of sex is not intimacy at all. The good thing about healthy sexuality is that it creates an obvious and ideal container for true intimacy, at least now and then. I wonder how a person who has never practiced risky self-disclosure with at least one other human being would know how to be intimate with God. I sincerely doubt the possibility. (Is this the real meaning of "nakedness"?) Both healthy celibacy and sexual encounter demand deep and true intimacy, and both can be the most effective avoidance of it. (And I write this after almost fifty years in a celibate community of men and after lots of counseling both given and received, and in a strangely sexualized world.)

Intimacy is not just a well-kept secret of the soul, not just a mystery that defies logic, not just a poverty that we avoid. I believe vulnerable intimacy is the entrance into and the linchpin between all human and divine love. It does not matter which comes first; it is just important that we pass through this gate of fear and find what lives inside us — and on the other side of the gate.

Intimate love is the true temple that we all desire. I guess you have to want to love and to be loved very badly—or we will never go to this strange temple and will never find our True Selves. So God obliges and created us in just that way, with a bottomless and endless need to be loved and to love. I end with a quote from John's too unquoted letter (1 John 4:8):

Everyone who loves is born of God and knows God,

Anyone who fails to love can never have known God,

For God is love.

CHAPTER 9

Love Is Stronger Than Death

 Make ready for the Christ, whose smile like lightning, sets free the song of ever-lasting glory that now sleeps—in your paper flesh.
THOMAS MERTON

So what does this book say to you? Is it as life changing and death shattering as I hoped? Does it deconstruct most religion and utterly reconstruct it at the same time? Does it lift heavy weights from your back and your heart? If I said it even half well, it should. If you heard it even halfway, it could. And it eventually will, because it names the way it is, and the eternal patterns will sooner or later show themselves, whether I say it well or not, or whether you hear it now or later.

William Stafford said all this, just about perfectly, in his rightly named poem and book of poems, "The Way It Is":

There's a thread you follow. It goes among
Things that change. But it doesn't change.
People wonder about what you are pursuing.
You have to explain about the thread.
But it is hard for others to see.
While you hold it you can't get lost.
Tragedies happen; people get hurt
or die; and you suffer and get old.
Nothing you do can stop time's unfolding.
You don't ever let go of the thread.[1]

My words for the thread that Stafford speaks of are the *True Self* — the immortal diamond that we have been mining here. Your True Self is who you are, and always have been in God, and at its core, it is love itself. Love is both who you are and who you are still becoming, like a sunflower seed that becomes its own sunflower. Most of human history has called the True Self your "soul" or "your participation in the eternal life of God." The great surprise and irony is that "you," or who you think you are, have nothing to do with its original creation or its demise. It's sort of disempowering and utterly empowering at the same time, isn't it? All you can do is nurture it, which is saying quite a lot. It is love becoming love in this unique form called "me."

It seems to be a fully cooperative effort according to St. Paul (Romans 8:28), and according to my own limited experience too. God never forces himself on us or coerces you toward life or love by any threats whatsoever. God seduces you, yes; coerces you, no (Jeremiah 20:7; Matthew 11:28–30). Whoever this God is, he or she is utterly free and utterly respects our own human freedom. Love cannot happen in any other way. Love flourishes inside freedom and then increases that freedom even more. "For freedom Christ has set us free!" shouts St. Paul in his critique of all legalistic religion (Galatians 5:1).

We are all allowed to ride life and love's wonderful mystery for a few years — until life and love reveal themselves as the same thing, which is the final and full message of the risen Christ — life morphing into a love that is beyond space and time. He literally "breathes" shalom and forgiveness into the universal air (John 20:22–23). You get to add your own finishing touches of love, your own life breath to the Great Breath, and then return the completed package to its maker in a brand-new but also same form. It is indeed the same "I," but now it is in willing union with the great "I AM" (Exodus 3:14). It is no longer just one but not two either.

As I hope you have heard scattered throughout this book, I believe the summary meaning of the Resurrection of Jesus is totally summed up in the climactic line from the Song of Songs (8:6) that I translate as *"love is stronger than death."* If the banner that the risen Christ usually holds in art should say anything, that is what it should say: *Amor vincit omnia!* Love will win! Love is all that remains. Love and life are finally the same thing, and you know that for yourself once you have walked through death.

Note that Stafford in his poem did not tell you not to let go of the thread, but rather that *"you don't ever let go of the thread."* Why? Because you can't. It has you. Love has you. Love *is* you. Love, and our deep need for love, alone recognizes love itself. Remember that you already are what you are seeking. Any fear "that your lack of fidelity could cancel God's fidelity, is absurd" (Romans 3:3), says the master teacher, Paul. Love has finally overcome fear, and your house is being rebuilt on a new and solid foundation. This foundation was always there, but it took us a long time to find it, for "It is love alone that lasts" (1 Corinthians 13:13). All you have loved in your life and been loved by is eternal and true, and not just other humans. Two of the primary images of final salvation are Noah's ark (Genesis 6:19) and "the Peaceable Kingdom" (Isaiah 11:6), and, interestingly enough, both are filled with images of animals—as worth saving and as images of paradise regained.

My fellow friar, Father Jack Wintz, has written a theologically solid book on why we can consider all things loved, loving, and lovable as participating in eternity, including animals.[2] What made us think we were the only ones who loved and are lovable? If unconditional love, loyalty, and obedience are the tickets to an eternal life, then my black Labrador, Venus, will surely be there long before me, along with all the dear animals in nature who care for their young at great cost to themselves and have suffered so much at the hands of humans. In some ways, the animals hold onto the thread of their destiny much more humbly and loyally than we do. The difference between humans and animals is that animals fully say yes to their being.[3] We usually don't—which is why I had to write this book.

MARY MAGDALENE

Did it ever surprise you that Christ appeared to Mary Magdalene first after his raising? She is the symbolic stand-in for all of longing humanity and all who are considered "sinners." All the many Marys of the Gospel seem to be summed up in her at this point, at least in our imaginal world.[4] Jesus says of the woman with the alabaster jar, perhaps Mary Magdalene, "Her many sins must have been forgiven her, or she would not have shown such great love." And then he turns it around and affirms the opposite also: "It is the person who is forgiven little who shows little love" (Luke 7:47). He is making an amazing connection that might be the heart of the matter here. He is rather clearly saying that *the very failures and radical insufficiency of our lives are what lead us into larger life and love.* He says, as it were, to the sneering men at that gathering, "You are all wrong about God! She gets it, and you don't!"

Do you realize how counterintuitive this is? Do you realize how hopeful this is? The human playing field is utterly leveled. It is our mistakes that lead us to God. We come to divine union not by doing it right but by doing it wrong, as we all most surely do. Mary Magdalene is the icon and archetype of love itself—*needed, given, received, and passed on*—and Jesus' appearance to her first and alone is the clear affirmation of this wonderful and astounding message. Only a history of interpretation by male celibate clergy was unable to see that which is now obvious.

Mary Magdalene is the Gospel personage who most needs love to be stronger than death, and so she is the first to know it—and perhaps at the deepest level. She is the first one who symbolically comes to "consciousness," as it were, and thus is the clear "witness to the witnesses." She is the real knower, and her *need* for love and forgiveness has made that to be true; in fact, love and knowledge have become one in her. No surprise that she is named as standing at the foot of the cross—with two more Marys (John 19:25)—who walked through the mystery with Jesus. And they were also the first ones at the tomb on Sunday.[5] Mary is the archetypal name for all those who live out of their True Selves and know its Source.

YES MUST PRECEDE NO

Most of us learned to say no without the deeper joy of yes. We were trained to put up with all the "dying" and just take it on the chin. Saying no to the False

Self does not necessarily please God or please anybody, and surely not you. There is too much resentment and self-pity involved in this kind of false dying. *There is a good dying and there is a bad dying.* Good dying is unto something bigger and better; bad dying is just damn stupid dying that profits nobody. It is too much no and not enough yes. You must hold out for yes! Don't be against anything unless you are much more for it first or for something else that is better. "I want you to be you, all of you, your best you!" is what true lovers say to one another, not just, "I do not like this about you," or, "Why don't you change that?" Sincerely caring for another person before trying to change him or her is the only way that person will change anyway.

God tries to first create a joyous yes inside you, far more than any kind of no. Then you have become God's full work of art, and for you, love is now stronger than death, and Christ is surely risen in you! Love and life have become the same thing. Just saying no is resentful dieting, whereas finding your deepest yes, and eating from that table, is always a spiritual banquet. You see, *death and no are the same thing. Love and yes are even more the same thing.*

The True Self does what it really loves and therefore loves whatever it does. I am sure that is what

Joseph Campbell meant by his oft misunderstood line, "Follow your bliss."

The risen Christ is a great big yes to everything (2 Corinthians 1:19), even its own earlier imperfect stages. The final stupendous gift is that your False Self has now become your True Self. That is precisely the metamorphosis that we call Resurrection. The risen Christ is still and forever the wounded Jesus — and yet so much more now. The raw material of every aspect of his life, of our life too, is not ended but merely changed. "This perishable nature will put on imperishability, and this mortal body will put on immortality" (1 Corinthians 15:52.54) — one including the other, not one in place of the other.

Very importantly, the risen Christ is beyond any limits of space and time, as revealed in his bilocation (Luke 24:32–39). He is a universal connection, intimate with everything. The one and the many have become the One. We operate now as a part of the "the biggest ecosystem" and not alone anymore.

I would say a very small percentage of Christians let the corporate Body of Christ carry both their goodness and their badness, *both the weight of their glory and the burden of their sin*, to use two of Paul's felicitous phrases. Western individualism has really done us in. It has created either ego-inflated or ego-deflated people or, more commonly, a daily seesaw between both—yet both of them are illusions. Neither your worthiness nor your unworthiness is yours alone, and it is a burden to try to maintain them as if they were. What a relief. This might be the very recipe for God's peace, which is *an underlying vastness and abundance that can absorb all negativity and watch it pass away*.

For the True Self, there is nothing to hate, reject, deny, or judge as unworthy or unnecessary. It has "been forgiven much and so it loves much" (Luke 7:47). Compassion and mercy come easily now, once you live from inside the Big Body of love. The detours of the False Self were all just delaying tactics, bumps in the road, pressure points that created something new in the long run, as pressure does to carbon deep beneath the earth. God uses everything to construct this hard and immortal diamond, our core of love. And diamonds, they say, are the hardest substance on this earth. It is this strong diamond of love that will always be stronger than death.

All, absolutely everything, is now made use of in this great economy of grace. "Grace is everywhere," Georges Bernanos said at the end of his novel and the end of his life.[6] You can now enjoy unearned love in yourself and allow it in everyone else too. This patient mining process will make you compassionate and forgiving with the unfinished diamonds of all the others who are on the same journey as you are. They have perhaps not been under the pressure or drawn by the force field of resurrection long enough yet.

Things like skin color, social class, ethnicity, sexual orientation, and even religion are now seen for the "accidents" that they are. Of themselves, they never reveal the love core, not even close. This True Self cannot find or know God without bringing everybody else along for the same ride. It is one great big finding and one great big being found, all at the same time.

Diamonds, once soft black carbon, become beautiful and radiant white lightning under pressure. The true pattern, the big secret, has now been revealed and exposed "like a treasure hidden in a field." You did not find the Great Love except by finding yourself too, and you cannot find your True Self without falling into the Great Love.

Diamonds are deeply hidden under miles, pounds, and pressure of earth and time, but like the True Self, like the thread, like the presence itself, they are there. And now YOU are there too.

My dear people,
We are already the children of God.
But what we are in the future is not yet fully revealed.
All we know, is that when it is revealed,
We shall all be like him [1 John 3:2].

Many Christians begin Lent on Ash Wednesday with the signing of ashes on their forehead and the words from Genesis 3:19, which is just the first shocking part of the message:

Dust you are, and unto dust you shall return.

But then we should be *anointed* ("Christed") with a holy oil on Easter morning with the other half of the message:

Love is always stronger than death, and unto that love you have now returned.

I order you, O sleeper, to awake!
I did not create you to be held a prisoner in hell.
Rise from the dead, for I am the life of the dead.
Rise up, work of my hands, you were created in my image.
Rise, let us leave this place, for you are in me and I am in you.
Together we form only one person and we cannot be separated!

FROM AN ANCIENT HOMILY ON HOLY SATURDAY, EASTER EVE

THE TRUE SELF AND THE FALSE SELF

This important distinction between true and false selves is so foundational that it is often overlooked, and also hard to teach. It is also hard for some to comprehend if they have never had experience of deep inner truth or inner falsity. Over years of retreat work, I have resorted to an almost simplistic geometric image, and for many it seems to help. It imprints in the imagination better than concepts do.

The only disagreement that ever arose was when some wanted me to put the "me" circle entirely inside and surrounded by the large "God/Reality" circle. For me, this is a mistake, and one that you cannot live up to. God creates, maintains, and respects the unique creation that you are—as you!

You are not entirely absorbed into God, and you are not the same as God, which would be pantheism. You are, however, inherently in union with God—and the relationship is continually given and offered from God's side. We can only accept being accepted — as we are — which is so difficult for the ego to do. It always feels like dying, and it is.

The True Self

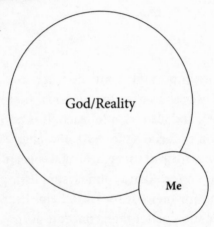

- Your absolute identity
- Your soul
- Who you are in God
- Who God is in you
- Inherently satisfied and content
- Feels and is immortal
- The Great Self, the Christ Self, the God Self, the Buddha Self, the "branch connected to the vine" (John 15:5)

The False Self

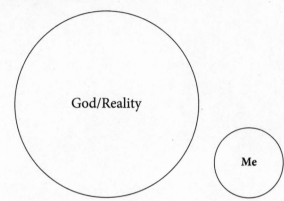

- Your relative identity
- Your "starter kit" at life
- The identity you created for yourself
- The self that changes and dies
- Inherently needy and fragile
- Living from the outside in
- Not bad or even "false" as much as passing
- Is self-enclosed and self-referential
- Dissatisfied and always reinventing itself
- The "small self" before transformation
- The "branch cut off from the vine" (John 15:4–5)
- The "single" grain of wheat (John 12:24)
- Precisely your *separate* self, as separate
- The illusion that must pass

A MOSAIC OF METAPHORS

This appendix sets out all of the Gospel metaphors in one place, so you can see them in one long glance and get the imaginal world that they summarily create. Images that strike you are probably calling for deeper meditation on them. They will give you soul access to the Mystery. You will see that the Resurrection accounts are not about "proving a miracle" (although I do not question the physical resurrection of Jesus) as much as *a joyous contagion* that is spreading around quickly and changing people. That is the message. In general, notice this:

1. The Risen Christ normally represents the True Self—the enlightened and transformed soul that is intimate with everything.

2.   The other players and images represent the various
     human attitudes that allow us to make contact with
     the True Self and where to look for the Mystery.

   • *Mark 16:1–20*: The Rising Sun. Rolling away
the stone. Absence before presence. "Going before you
into Galilee." Fear response. First ending was lost or
deliberately torn out? Appears first to the recovering
"sinner" and a woman. Refusal to believe is the norm.
The disciples are reproached. Tells them to give this
message to "all of creation," not just humans.
   • *Matthew 27:57–28:20*: Vigilant waiting by two
Marys, "sitting opposite death." The secular system
wants to block any possibility of resurrection. First
day of a new week of creation. An earthquake. Awe,
joy, excitement. Jesus running into the future. Women
get it; "hesitation" by the men. Religion itself tries to
deny and buy off the message. Jesus takes the initiative
toward them twice. Tell "all the nations," so not a
closed society. Universal and timeless presence.
   • *Luke 24*: Absence that is presence. Terror.
Announcement of life over death. Women believe;
men think it is "pure nonsense." Emmaus journey:
How you are present to others is how you are
present to God. Ongoing incarnational message in

the breaking of bread and eating fish. Jesus waits to be invited but accepts. Contrast between ghostly presence and physical eating. Joy. Ascension as the very last movement and message (also in Acts 1:9–12): Spirit as "power" and empowering "to the ends of the earth." "Why are you staring into the sky?" Get back to earth!

• *John 20 and 21*: First day of the week. New creation of light. Centrality of Mary Magdalene. John and Peter running to the tomb: love arrives before role. The new Ark of the Covenant, with angels presiding over the space that is both absence and full presence. "Do not cling to me." Both form and formlessness at the same time. Behind closed doors, which he passes through, implying a different kind of embodiment. Joy, peace, breath, forgiveness, and the Holy Spirit, all conflated as one event. Touching the physical wounds is the way to faith. A new charcoal fire. Three denials reversed and undone. "My God and your God too"; the One who raised me will raise you. Great catch of fish — 153 symbolizing all the known nations and a world of grace and abundance. Love means both servanthood and surrender, the head apostle is told. In the second half of life, Peter must allow himself to be led "where he would rather not go."

Transfiguration Images

I believe that the three Gospel versions of Jesus' "trans-figuration" are actually a misplaced resurrection scene, deliberately placed in the middle of the narrative to make an important point. There are needed "moun-taintop moments" in the middle of life that help us hold on and hold out for the final and full momentous life (Matthew 17:1–9; Mark 9:2–10; Luke 9:28–36). You need to touch upon your True Self in *this* world first. In each rendition of the story, the transfiguration experience is something the disciples want to hold onto, but they must go back down the mountain into ordinary life. They are told not to say a word of it to anyone; the experience is unspeakable to those who have never been there, it seems.

- *Mark 9:2–8, Matthew 17:1–8, Luke 9:28–36*: Mountaintop experience inner group ready, but still has to be led there, dazzling white/all colors, Jesus is a "Third Something" integrating the law and the prophets, a "mandala" of enlightenment, fright, "heavy with sleep but kept awake and saw his glory"(Luke 9:32), yet a "cloud of unknowing," mountaintop clarity and shadow at the same time, divine experience of beloved status, wonder and desire to hold onto it, temptation to build "tents" of enclosure, "do not be afraid." In the end, Jesus stands alone; they are unable to talk about it, actually can't talk about it because ineffable, back down the mountain into life as usual. "How do we now put the two worlds together into one world?" and "How do we enter the orbit of wholeness with Jesus, Moses, and Elijah?" seem to be desires that the reader is left with.

WATCHING AT THE TOMB: ATTITUDES FOR PRAYER

Now Mary Magdalene and another Mary kept vigil there, seated opposite the tomb.
MATTHEW 27:61

Picture yourself, like Mary Magdalene, sitting outside the tomb of the buried Christ. It is the ultimate luminal space, the Sabbath of Sabbaths, the time of ultimate rest and waiting: the Saturday between Good Friday and Easter Sunday.

Many fruitful possibilities and entranceways are offered here. Read the list below, and try the practices that most invite or challenge you today. These might help you find your attention and your inner silence. Let it be your guiding metaphor for a good twenty-minute "sit" as you also keep vigil:

- Sitting in love.
- Filling the tragic gap with pure presence, often in the presence of "nothing" or even "death."
- Note that Mary does not keep vigil alone. Prayer often needs other "Marys" for support, as we see in this text.
- Waiting without answers.
- Hoping without evidence.
- Love sustaining itself by longing.
- Inner space is only created by patient watching.
- The "grief work" of holding patiently, without resolution or consolation.
- Prayer as watching and waiting more than doing.
- Prayer as unknowing and not knowing.
- Prayer of quiet (no talking mentioned).
- Christ in the tomb is still the Christ (absence is its own kind of presence).
- The dead Christ is still Christ. What does that connote for you? How often do you intentionally pray in the presence of a "dead" situation?
- An exercise in not forcing resurrection but letting it come when it will.

- Note that a "large stone is across the entranceway" but they do not try to move it.
- The dead Christ is your passing display of negativity, anger, fear, lust, and hopelessness, and you attachment to these deaths.

You must stay in your vigil until the dead Christ resurrects, that is, until you can release or detach from the reactions of your False Self. This may take two minutes or two hours.

HEAD INTO HEART:
"THE SACRED HEART"

Many have described prayer as bringing your thinking down into your heart. This is not just sentimentality. It was almost the preoccupation of much of Orthodox monasticism, as we see in classics like the Philokalia and the teachings of the Desert Fathers and Mothers. It always seemed like soft piety to me until someone taught me how to do it, and I learned the immense benefits of doing it. Probably the best single teacher for me — on the how — was Robert Sardello in his little masterpiece of a book, *Silence: The Mystery of Wholeness*.[1]

As a Catholic, I was often puzzled by the continued return to heart imagery among our saints and in our art. The "Sacred Heart" of Jesus and the "Immaculate Heart of Mary" are images known to

Catholics worldwide, where they are always pointing to their heart and it is ablaze. I often wonder what people actually do with these images. Are they mere sentiment? Are they objects of worship or objects of transformation? *Such images keep recurring only if they are speaking something important and good from the unconscious,* maybe even something necessary for the soul's emergence. What might that be?

Next time a resentment, negativity, or irritation comes into your mind, for example, and you want to play it out or attach to it, *move that thought or person literally into your heart space* because such commentaries are almost entirely lodged in your head. There, surround it with silence (which is much easier to do in the heart). There, it is surrounded with blood, which will often feel warm like coals. In this place, it is almost impossible to comment, judge, create story lines, or remain antagonistic. You are in a place that does not create or feed on contraries but is the natural organ of life, embodiment, and love. Love lives and thrives in the heart space. It has kept me from wanting to hurt people who have hurt me. It keeps me every day from obsessive, repetitive, or compulsive head games. It can make the difference between being happy and being miserable and negative.

Could this be what we are really doing when we say we are praying for someone? *Yes, we are holding them in our heart space. Do it in an almost physical sense, and you will see how calmly and quickly it works.* Now the Sacred Heart and the Immaculate Heart have been transferred to you. They are pointing for you to join them there. The "sacred heart" is then your heart too.

ADAM'S BREATHING: PRAYING FROM THE CLAY

God breathed into the clay of the earth and it became a living being (adamah).
GENESIS 2:7

When we cannot choose words in order to pray properly, the Spirit expresses our pleas in ways that could never be put into words ... and these pleas are according to the mind of God.
ROMANS 8:26–27

A full prayer must draw from both breath and clay, from above and outside, and also equally from below and within. It must have *both inspiration and embodied energy.* We have emphasized the first up to now, but not the second.

Mental Prayer

Our first concept of prayer is usually top down, with grace from above and outer animation from a transcendent God "breathing" into us. This is a good start.

In asking for grace, invoking your Higher Power, through words, waiting for "the descent of the dove" as it were, still leaves God mostly "out there" and not also "in here." This spiritual imbalance was balanced out by the Incarnation of God into flesh (John 1:14) and the gift of the Indwelling Spirit (Romans 5:5).

So if the Incarnation is true and we are the Body of Christ, then prayer is fully experienced when it is also from the bottom up, when we "pray from the clay," at the energetic, cellular level too. *Adam (and Eve!) must receive and breathe the breath of Yahweh for themselves.* Only then are humans, composed of both breath and clay, "all systems go"!

Body Prayer

We must hunker down into the "Body of Hope and Resurrection" (Philippians 3:9–11; 1 Corinthians 15:44) and pray also from below and from within, on a cellular and energetic level too — or the attitude of prayer does not last or go deep.

- You are not thinking your prayer as much as energetically feeling your prayer.
- You pay attention from the bottom up and from the inside out.
- Rest into the Body of Christ energy instead of trying to pull an Infinite God into your finite world.
- Your body itself receives *and knows,* and is indeed "a temple" (1 Corinthians 3:16–17) where God dwells in the Spirit.
- Walking meditation, yoga, and breathing exercises are all helpful here.

Body prayer actually works much more quickly and more naturally than thought prayer alone.

Body prayer is what we have tried to do with inspiring music, body gestures, and all sacraments, so this is not a new idea. It is what many are seeking in tai chi, pilgrimages, prayer beads, chanting, repeating the Jesus Prayer until it prays itself in us and through us, and so on.

To "pray from the clay" will also move you to the shared level of prayer. You will know that "you" are not doing the prayer, but you *are falling into the unified field*, and the Body of Christ is now praying through you (Romans 8:26–27) and with you. It becomes "our" prayer, and not just my prayer. Now you pray not so much *to* Christ as much as *through* Christ, and you will know experientially that you are Christ's Body too.

The resolution of the false dilemma of high Christology and low Christology now becomes an inner Christ consciousness, combining the best of both and resolving the common conflict between conservatives and liberals.

TWELVE WAYS TO PRACTICE RESURRECTION NOW

1. Refuse to identify with negative, blaming, antagonistic, or fearful thoughts (you cannot stop "having" them).

2. Apologize when you hurt another person or situation.

3. Undo your mistakes by some positive action toward the offended person or situation.

4. Do not indulge or believe your False Self—that which is concocted by your mind and society's expectations.

5. Choose your True Self—your radical union with God—as often as possible throughout the day.

6. Always seek to change yourself before trying to change others.

7. Choose as much as possible to serve rather than be served.

8. Whenever possible, seek the common good over your mere private good.

9. Give preference to those in pain, excluded, or disabled in any way.

10. Seek just systems and policies over mere charity.

11. Make sure your medium is the same as your message.

12. Never doubt that it is all about love in the end.

A *note on Bible versions*: I studied from the *Jerusalem Bible*, I have made use of the *New American Bible*, and I often read *The Message* to get a new slant on a passage, but the edited form I use is often my own translation or a combination of the versions I have noted.

Invitation

1. I will use Aldous Huxley's definition of "the perennial philosophy" from his book *The Perennial Philosophy* (New York: HarperCollins, 1944) as an adequate definition of my own understanding of the same: "The metaphysic that recognizes a divine Reality substantial to the world of things and lives and minds; the psychology that finds in the soul something similar to, or even identical with, divine Reality, and the ethic that places man's final end in the knowledge of the immanent and transcendent Ground of all being. This is immemorial and universal" (vi).

2. The significant Scripture here, if Scripture helps you, is the hymn at the beginning of Colossians (1:15–20). Here we are not just talking about the historic Jesus as much as a cosmic figure who "recapitulates" the meaning of creation and is fully identified with Jesus—and, further, Jesus accepts this role and its implications. This is a far

more universal notion of the very tribal Jesus than most Christians seem to have today. I will call this *the Cosmic Christ* (Ephesians 1:3–14 makes the same claim).

3. Julia Esqivel, "Threatened with Resurrection," in *Threatened with Resurrection: Prayers and Poems from an Exiled Guatemalan Woman* (1982 Spanish edition).

Preface

1. Jaroslav Pelikan, *The Vindication of Tradition: The 1983 Jefferson Lecture in the Humanitie*s (New Haven, Conn.: Yale University Press, 1984), 65.

2. In the foundational methodology of my own teaching, I eventually realized that personal experience is the dynamic third that is in effect anyway; and now must be consciously examined and critiqued to get us beyond the largely useless Scripture-versus-tradition dilemma. History has seen the Catholics misuse tradition and the Protestants misuse Scripture, with neither of them accountable for their de facto "subjectivity," biases, and personal experience in regard to both Scripture and tradition. This is the basic methodology for our Living School starting in Albuquerque in 2013 (see cac.org) and is stated in this way: "Scripture as validated by experience, and experience as validated by Tradition, are good scales for one's worldview." Then we must use critical reason to coordinate these three.

3. Richard Rohr, *The Naked Now* (Chestnut Ridge, N.Y.: Crossroad Publishing, 2009). This entire book is about nondual consciousness, but Chapters Twelve through

Fourteen might particularly be helpful in helping us see that prayer is more a life stance than saying words. Whatever you do in conscious union and love is prayer.

4. Ken Wilber, *One Taste* (Boston: Shambhala, 2000), 25–28. Wilber's brilliant distinction between the translative and transformative functions of religion is presented in many places, but nowhere more concisely and clearly than here. My experience after forty years as a priest is that the vast majority of religion is *translative* (communicates values to the old self) and only occasionally *transformative* (actually changes the self at its core). This is much of my thesis in this whole book.

5. Thomas Aquinas, *Summa Theologica*, "*De Anima*," II, 37.

6. Read the book of Wisdom 11:23–12:1 if you want a magnificent and poetic statement of this belief. It rearranged my life vision when I first read it as a young man.

Chapter One: What Is "The True Self"?

1. Augustine, *Confessions*, X, 38 (or 27 in some translations).

2. This quote from Matthew 22:14, although found nowhere else, got an awful (read terrible!) lot of mileage in Christian circles to teach an exclusionary and scarcity model of Jesus' teaching. Most are convinced that verses 11 to 14 were almost certainly added to the inclusive parable by a later scribe who did not like the inclusionary and nondual nature of verses 9 and 10. He created a silly myth of wedding garments along with generations of people "weeping and grinding their teeth" after they tried to make sense of this indecipherable verse. Luke's

version in 14:15–24 is undoubtedly closer to the original inclusive Jesus. What hope is there if I am not one of the "chosen" ones? There is some anti-Gospel hidden inside the Gospel, just like life itself. Even the call here is not to "all" but just to "many," which probably implies Matthew's Jewish audience. But the inclusive Jesus still shines through.

3. Richard Rohr, *Falling Upward* (San Francisco: Jossey-Bass, 2011). My thesis in this entire book is that there are two halves of life with significantly different central tasks. If you get your "container" in the first half of life, then you are ready for the "contents" that the container was meant to hold.

4. The anointing symbol needs more than a small footnote, but let me try anyway. Anointing became the standing *Christ* symbol ("The Anointed One") for the confluence of matter and Spirit. The Jewish longing for "The Anointed One" (*Messiah*) is absolutely correct and also universal. It is only much later applied to Jesus of Nazareth, who became for Christians the living embodiment of True Self, where human and divine coexist. It all starts here with Jacob and a stone and an epiphany that built a ladder between heaven and earth. Wherever you find such a "stone," you have found the beginnings of the Eternal Christ Mystery, you have found your Messiah.

5. I know this from years of teaching young people and from the phenomenal worldwide response to the Enneagram, which I learned in 1973, and also from tools like the Myers-Briggs personality indicator. Both open up

a huge and real inner world through the door of self-knowledge—and to many people who would otherwise be bored by any talk of "spirituality" or interiority as something real or helpful. It is both sad and strange that many Christians think of such doorways as "mere psychology." Richard Rohr, *The Enneagram: A Christian Perspective* (Chestnut Ridge, N.Y.: Crossroad Publishing, 2001).

6. Rohr, *Falling Upward* (where I try to say this is a first-half-of-life problem).

7. Thomas Merton, *Love and Living* (Orlando, Fla.: Harcourt, 1979), 11–12.

8. For more information, see "Spiral Dynamics" through its various interpreters, like Don Beck, Chris Cowan, Ken Wilber (who calls his own more comprehensive version "Integral Theory"), and the German school, which is applying it to spirituality in books like Marion Küstenmacher, Tilmann Haberer, and Werner Tiki Küstenmacher's *Gott 9.0* (Munich: Guetersloher Verlagshaus, 2010)

9. Richard Rohr, *Adam's Return: The Five Promises of Male Initiation* (Chestnut Ridge, N.Y.: Crossroad Publishing, 2004) 155–157.

10. I recommend a teacher like Martin Laird, OSA, who will show you how you allow your attention to be stolen by endless mental commentary, judgments, and creating self-serving story lines—which we dare to call "thinking." Both of his books, *Into the Silent Land* (New York: Oxford University Press, 2006) and *A Sunlit Absence*

(New York: Oxford University Press, 2011), are excellent examples of the recovery of the older contemplative practice for Christians. A masterpiece of a book in this regard is Robert Sardello's *Silence: The Mystery of Wholeness* (Benson, N.C.: Goldenstone Press, 2006), which I make use of in Appendix D.

11. Gerard Manley Hopkins, "As Kingfishers Catch Fire," in *Mortal Beauty, God's Grace* (New York: Random House, 2003), 23.

12. Rohr, *Adam's Return*. This is the core message of any authentic initation rite, 60–66.

13. Teresa of Avila, *Interior Castle*, I, 2.

14. Richard Rohr, *The Naked Now* (Chestnut Ridge, N.Y.: Crossroad Publishing, 2009), chap. 2. Even the sacred name Yahweh is the sound of inhalation and exhalation. Now we know why so many teachers just said, "Pay attention to the breath."

15. Pseudo-Dionysius, "The Divine Names" (3:1), *The Complete Works* (New York: Paulist Press, 1987), 68.

Chapter Two: What Is "The False Self"?

1. Kathleen Dowling Singh, *The Grace in Dying* (New York: HarperCollins, 2000), 15. I find her conclusions from years of hospice work brilliant, courageous, and life changing. *The Grace in Dying* could well be read as a companion to this book.

2. Stephen Levine, *Who Dies? An Investigation of Conscious Living and Conscious Dying* (New York: Doubleday,

1982), 182. In a more Buddhist style, Levine's book is a true description of what Christians are ritually proclaiming when they say, "Christ has died, Christ is Risen, and Christ will come again." He knew how to say it in a more neutral way.

3. James Hillman, *We've Had a Hundred Years of Psychotherapy—and the World's Getting Worse* (New York: HarperCollins, 1992).

4. Richard Rohr, *Falling Upward* (San Francisco: Jossey-Bass, 2011), 25.

5. Richard Rohr, *Breathing Under Water* (Cincinnati, Ohio: Franciscan Media, 2011), 21–24.

6. Ken Wilber, *One Taste* (Boston: Shambhala, 2000), 25–28.

7. Richard Rohr, *Emotional Sobriety* (Albuquerque, N.M., 2011). CD. http://cacradicalgrace.org.

8. Levine, *Who Dies?* 29.

9. Flannery O'Connor, "Revelation," in *The Complete Stories* (New York: Farrar, Straus and Giroux, 1971), 488–509.

10. Thomas Aquinas, *Summa Theologica*, III, q.8.3.

11. Thomas Merton, *New Seeds of Contemplation* (New York: New Directions, 1962), 227.

Chapter Three: What Dies and Who Lives?

1. Kathleen Dowling Singh, *The Grace in Dying* (New York: HarperCollins, 2000), 219

2. Daniel Ladinsky, *I Heard God Laughing: Renderings of Hafiz* (Walnut Creek, Calif.: Sufism Reoriented, 1996), 13.

3. T. S. Eliot, "Little Gidding, IV," in *Four Quartets* (San Diego, Calif.: Harcourt Brace, 1971).

Chapter Four: The Knife Edge of Experience

1. Goodness, truth, and unity were called "the transcendentals" and were seen as the inherent quality of Being Itself. In the Franciscan school of theology, we could speak of all being in a univocal way (with one voice) from God to humans to animals to trees to water. They all participate in Absolute Being in varying degrees. John Duns Scotus, OFM, taught that the opposite of good was not bad but nonbeing itself. The opposite of truth was not falsity but nonbeing itself. And the opposite of unity was not multiplicity but nonbeing itself. All the opposites are all held and contained within pure being, even the finite and the infinite, matter and Spirit, male and female, etc., and this harmony between things is called *beauty*, which for some is a fourth transcendental itself. This worldview creates a very positive theology and anthropology based on original blessing instead of original sin. It also creates a philosophical basis for nondual thinking and the nature of evil. Evil is nonbeing and unconsciousness. Beauty is the fullness of being and full consciousness.

2. Hubert Dreyfus and Sean Kelly, *All Things Shining* (New York: Free Press, 2011). In this insightful postmodern search for meaning, the authors make the case that some ancient peoples seem to have lived with a greater sense of wonder, gratitude, and inherent belonging than we do. Our individualism and autonomy no longer allow us to believe or enjoy that our heroism flows *through* us and

not so much *from* us. Self-assertion is perhaps not as important as listening, allowing, trusting, and belonging. Today we go to science for objective "truth," and we go to religion for enduring meaning. Yet they should not be in competition with one another.

3. Thomas Merton, *The Journals of Thomas Merton* (New York: HarperCollins, 1999), 7:323.

4. Sallie McFague, *The Body of God: An Ecological Theology* (Minneapolis, Minn.: Fortress, 1993). Many similar books have emerged in the past twenty years, but this is one of the best, along with Ilia Delio's *The Emergent Christ* (Maryknoll, N.Y.: Orbis Books, 2011) and *Christ in Evolution* (Maryknoll, N.Y.: Orbis Books, 2008). Such thinking, often from women, is surely Christianity coming to maturity.

5. Richard Rohr, *Christ, Cosmology, and Consciousness* (Albuquerque, N.M., 2010). CD. cacradicalgrace.org.

6. Anthony of the Desert, *The Letters of St. Anthony the Great*, "Letter 6," trans. Derwas Chitty, June 1978.

7. Rosemary Haughton, *The Knife Edge of Experience* (London: Darton, Longman & Todd, 1972).

8. C. G. Jung, *AION: Researches into the Phenomenology of the Self* (Princeton, N.J.: Princeton University Press, 1979).

9. St. Irenaeus (125–203), *The Scandal of the Incarnation*, and St. Athanasius (297–373), *On the Incarnation*, are two early classics that set a bar of good theology that we have since seldom matched or even understood. The

mystery of incarnation is the unique trump card that Christianity adds to the deck of world religions.

10. John A. T. Robinson, *In the End God* (New York: Harper-Collins, 1968). This classic first helped me understand what endless life and resurrection might really mean when I first read it shortly before my ordination in 1970.

11. Matthew Fox, *Original Blessing* (New York: Tarcher, 2000). This book was groundbreaking for many Christians, and it well deserves to be. Although it is much more representative of the Perennial, Franciscan, and Native traditions, we are all grateful that it was a Dominican who brought this essential truth forward.

12. Mary Beth Ingham, *The Harmony of Goodness: Mutuality and Moral Living According to John Duns Scotus* (Quincy, Ill.: Franciscan Press, 1996).

13. Simone Weil, *Gravity and Grace* (London: Routledge, 1952), 3.

Chapter Five: Thou Art That

1. Richard Rohr, *The Naked Now* (Chestnut Ridge, N.Y.: Crossroad Publishing, 2009).

2. Richard Rohr, *The Divine Dance* (Albuquerque, N.M., 2009), CD, a recorded conference on the Trinity and its massive implications for all interfaith dialogue. It makes one indeed think that we are still in the very early stages of unpacking the Christian religion.

3. The phrase *prevenient grace* was coined by St. Augustine, who knew from St. Paul that grace exists prior to and

without reference to anything humans may have done or can do, "or grace would not be grace at all" (Romans 11:6 and Ephesians 2:8–10).

4. Marcus J. Borg, *Meeting Jesus Again for the First Time* (San Francisco: HarperSanFrancisco, 1994). Few contemporary teachers have unpacked the assumptions, the vision, and the teaching of Jesus with greater clarity and readability than Borg. He will liberate you for much bigger and more demanding truth.

5. Irenaeus of Lyons, *Against Heresies*, III, 10.2 (Paris: Sources Chrétiennes, Chef).

6. Meister Eckhart, *The Essential Sermons* (Mahwah, N.J.: Paulist Press, 1981).

7. Eckhart, *The Essential Sermons*.

8. Jorge Ferrer and Jacob Sherman (Eds.), *The Participatory Turn: Spirituality, Mysticism, and Religious Studies* (Albany, N.Y.: SUNY Press, 2008).

9. Owen Barfield, *Saving the Appearances* (New York: Harcourt Brace, 1957). Karl Jaspers, *The Origin and Goal of History* (New Haven, Conn.: Yale University Press, 1953). For an excellent analysis of where this is leading us, read Ewert Cousins, *Christ of the 21st Century* (Rockport, Mass.: Element, 1992).

10. Richard Rohr, *The Great Chain of Being* (Albuquerque, N.M., 2009). CD. cacradicalgrace.org.

11. Michael Christensen and Jeffery Wittung (Eds.), *Partakers of the Divine Nature* (Madison, N.J.: Fairleigh Dickinson University Press, 2007). This excellent collection will

give you the history, loss, and development of the theme of "deification" in the Christian tradition.

12. If you want to do your own research here, the fathers of the church to study are St. Clement of Alexandria, Origen, St. Basil, St. Athanasius and St. Irenaeus in the West, St. Gregory Nazianzen, St Gregory of Nyssa, St. Maximus the Confessor, Pseudo Macarius, Diadochus, and St. Gregory Palamas in the East. The primary texts are in the *Philokalia* collection and the teachings of the Hesychastic monks.

13. Pope John Paul II, "*Orientale Lumen*," Apostolic Letter of May 2, 1995, I:6.

Chapter Six: If It Is True, It Is True Everywhere

1. Bonaventure, "The Soul's Journey to God," in *Classics of Western Spirituality* (New York: Paulist Press 1978), V, 8.

2. Vincent of Lerin, *Commonitorium* (Cambridge: Cambridge University Press, 1915), #3.

3. Teilhard de Chardin, *The Divine Milieu* (New York: HarperCollins, 1960), and *The Phenomenon of Man* (New York: HarperCollins, 1975). Many people who have been deeply touched by these books have said to me something to this effect: "I could not repeat exactly what he taught me, but it changed my life!" I would say Teilhard had the same effect on me when I first read him in college in the early 1960s. It is hard to ever be small again after you have read Chardin.

Chapter Seven: Enlightenment at Gunpoint

1. Kathleen Dowling Singh, *The Grace in Dying* (New York: HarperCollins, 2000), 107.

2. Richard Rohr, *Adam's Return* (Chestnut Ridge, N.Y.: Crossroad Publishing, 2004).

3. I was writing this section on a late February day in 2012 and waxing eloquent about my belief that the Holy Spirit is a force field, similar to an electromagnetic or gravitational field. When you are aligned in love, you can expect lots of coincidences, providences, "usings," and synchronicities in your life. I pointed out how Paul also resorted to body metaphors when he described sin and death (Romans 7:23–24), life and resurrection (Philippians 3:9–12, 3:21), and also our mutual connectedness in walking the whole path as an organism "body of Christ" (1 Corinthians 12:12–27). All of these seemed to have a shared, embodied, material character to them. That is my experience. But then I got scared, and thought you would all consider me flaky, new age, or unorthodox, and stopped writing with great discouragement. I tried to distract myself by checking my e-mail, and in five seconds I pulled up an attachment from a recent theological acquaintance at a conference. He was sending me his doctoral thesis, with full permission to delete it if I was not interested. There on the screen appeared a title I had never seen before: "The Holy Spirit as a Field of Force in the Theology of Wolfhart Pannenberg"! I sincerely thank Theodore James Whapham for allowing me to tell you

this story, and for his cooperation with the force field of the Holy Spirit on a February 28, 2012, afternoon. You see why I believe that resurrection has to be described in material terms too. I personally believe that we confused these living, real, and highly operative organisms with organizations and created many highly structured church institutions in lieu of learning how to "discern the spirits" of life and death.

4. C. G. Jung, *AION: Researches into the Phenomenology of the Self* (Princeton, N.J.: Princeton University Press, 1979), 9ii, esp. para. 271 and 283.

5. John Polkinghorne, *Science and the Trinity: The Christian Encounter with Reality* (New Haven, Conn.: Yale University Press, 2004). Books such as this are multiplying rapidly now, and I offer this as one excellent example. Jesus' statement seems to apply again in our time: "You know how to read the face of the sky but you do not know how to read the signs of the times" (Matthew 16:3). Both reveal the same patterns of change, death, and resurrection.

6. Richard Rohr, *Things Hidden* (Cincinnati, Ohio: Franciscan Media, 2008). There was no "price" to be paid except perhaps *to* our closed minds, our inability to believe that God could love us unconditionally, 185–205.

7. Mary Beth Ingham, *Scotus for Dunces* (St. Bonaventure, N.Y.: Franciscan Institute, 2003), 75ff. Following John Duns Scotus' lead, we Franciscans were the minority position inside of medieval Catholicism on the issue

of atonement. Most Protestants unknowingly just followed the majority position that Jesus "had" to die for our sins to pay some cosmic debt. Fortunately, the minority position is now being broadly affirmed in our time.

8. Richard Rohr, *Breathing Under Water* (Cincinnati, Ohio: Franciscan Media, 2011). In the final chapter of this book, "Only a Suffering God Can Save," I address the issue of evil and human suffering and God's involvement or noninvolvement.

9. Karl Rahner, *The Trinity* (Chestnut Ridge, N.Y.: Crossroad Publishing, 1999), 10.

10. Paul Fiddes, *Participating in God: A Pastoral Doctrine of the Trinity* (Louisville, Ky.: Westminster, 2000). This book is an excellent example of a growing field of teachers who are unpacking the endless implications of God as relationship itself.

11. Catherine LaCugna, *God for Us* (San Francisco: HarperSanFrancisco, 1973). This landmark book gives the history of the development of the doctrine of God as Trinity.

Chapter Eight: Intimate with Everything

1. Ilia Delio, *The Humility of God* (Cincinnati, Ohio: Franciscan Media, 2005). I could not stop highlighting and underlining this book by a dear Franciscan Sister friend and scholar.

2. II Vatican Council, *Dogmatic Constitution on Divine Revelation* (Dei Verbum), 1, #2–5.

3. What often seemed like pious Catholic sentimentality, the image of "the Sacred Heart," has eventually shown itself in my own life, and many others, to be much deeper and healing then I first imagined. The findings of the "HeartMath Solution" and Robert Sardello's magnificent unpacking of how the heart "holds" things in ways that the mind cannot, makes me realize how the mystics again intuited and imaged so correctly. Robert Sardello, *Silence* (Benson, N.C.: Goldenstone Press, 2006).

4. Richard Rohr, "Fear of Self-Disclosure," *Unpacking Paradoxes*, Dec. 28, 2011, http://richardrohr.wordpress .com/

5. Richard Rohr, *The Gates of the Temple: Sexuality and Spirituality* (Albuquerque, N.M., 2005). CD.

Chapter Nine: Love Is Stronger Than Death

1. William Stafford, *The Way It Is* (St. Paul, Minn.: Graywolf Press, 1977), 42.

2. Jack Wintz, *Will I See My Dog in Heaven?* (Brewster, Mass.: Paraclete Press, 2009). This book is not lightweight, and I am proud of my Franciscan brother for having the courage and the humility to be "considered" lightweight in writing it! He is not.

3. Eckhart Tolle, *Guardians of Being* (Novato, Calif.: New World Library, 2009). Tolle has the ability to take contemplation, incarnation, and resurrection to their logical, spiritual, and universal conclusions. What makes us think resurrection is just about us?

4. Cynthia Bourgeault, *The Meaning of Mary Magdalene* (Boston: Shambhala, 2010).

5. I hope this is not shocking or disappointing to Catholics and the Orthodox, who are beneficiaries of a developed theology of Mary, the Mother of Jesus. But we must be honest and admit that this has not developed in the New Testament period. In the scriptural witness itself, Mary Magdalene is the full icon of the message, especially because she was not made "ever a virgin" and "immaculately conceived" by later centuries. Although this might well be objectively true, it did push Mary the Mother of Jesus beyond the pale of imitation, or even identification. She could only be "worshiped," which is what Protestants refused to do. We probably did Mary of Nazareth little favor by pushing her so high, and we did most women little favor too. Mary already knew that "all generations will call me blessed" (Luke 1:48), and maybe we can return to that blessedness now in a new way, for she also said of herself that she was a "lowly handmaid" (1:47, 52) and uses the word *mercy* three times to describe God's relationship to her (1:49, 54, 55). She did not ask for, want, or need the pedestal we gave her. She already has it forever.

6. Georges Bernanos, *The Diary of a Country Priest* (New York: Carroll & Graf, 1937). These are the final words of the book, surely one of the most influential novels I ever read. It is sometimes translated as, "All is Grace," and is reported also to have been the final words of St. Therese of Lisieux in 1897.

Appendix D

1. Robert Sardello, *Silence: The Mystery of Wholeness* (Benson, N.C.: Goldenstone Press, 2006). I highly recommend the whole book, and particularly Chapter Eight, "The Silence of the Heart."

Alison, James. *The Joy of Being Wrong: Original Sin Through Easter Eyes*. Chestnut Ridge, N.Y.: Crossroad Publishing, 1959.

Alison, James. *Raising Abel: The Recovery of the Eschatological Imagination*. Chestnut Ridge, N.Y.: Crossroad Publishing, 1996.

Barnhart, Bruno. *Second Simplicity: The Inner Shape of Christianity*. Mahwah, N.J.: Paulist Press, 1999.

Becker, Ernest. *The Denial of Death*. New York: Free Press, 1973.

Bell, Rob. *Love Wins*, Harper Collins, 2011.

Benner, David G. *Spirituality and the Awakening Self*. Ada, Mich.: Baker Publishing, 2012.

Berman, Phillip L. *The Journey Home*. New York: Simon & Schuster, 1996.

Berthold, George C. *Maximus Confessor: Selected Writings*. Mahwah, N.J.: Paulist Press, 1985.

Bourgeault, Cynthia. *Mystical Hope*. Lanham, Md.: Rowman and Littlefield, 2001.

Bourgeault, Cynthia. *The Wisdom of Jesus*. Boston: Shambhala, 2008.

Bourgeault, Cynthia. *The Meaning of Mary Magdalene*. Boston: Shambhala, 2010.

Chardin, Teilhard de. *The Divine Milieu*. New York: Harper-Collins, 1960.

Christensen, Michael J., and Wittung, Jeffery A. *Partakers of the Divine Nature*. Cranbury, N.J.: Associated University Presses.

Clement, Olivier. *The Roots of Christian Mysticism*. London: New City, 1993.

Crosby, Michael H. *Repair My House: Becoming a "Kingdom" Catholic*. Maryknoll, N.Y.: Orbis Books, 2012.

Crossan, John Dominic, and Wright, N. T. *The Resurrection of Jesus*. Minneapolis, Minn.: Augsburg Fortress Press, 2006.

Delio, Ilia. *Christ in Evolution*. Maryknoll, N.Y.: Orbis Books, 2008.

Delio, Ilia. *The Emergent Christ*. Maryknoll, N.Y.: Orbis Books, 2011.

Delio, Ilia. *A Franciscan View of Creation: Learning to Live in a Sacramental World*. St. Bonaventure, N.Y.: Franciscan Institute, St. Bonaventure University, 2003.

Dourley, John P. *The Psyche as Sacrament*. Toronto: Inner City Books, 1981.

Dreyfus, Hubert, and Dorrance Kelly, Sean. *All Things Shining*. New York: Free Press, 2011.

Edinger, Edward F. *The Christian Archetype*. Toronto: Inner City Books, 1987.

Farley, Wendy. *Gathering Those Driven Away*. Louisville, Ky.: Westminster John Knox Press, 1958.

Ferguson, Everett, Malherbe, Abraham J., and Meyendorff, John. *Gregory of Nyssa: The Life of Moses*. Mahwah, N.J.: Paulist Press, 1978.

Fiddes, Paul S. *Participating in God*. Louisville, Ky.: Westminster John Knox Press, 2000.

Finley, James. *Merton's Palace of Nowhere*. Notre Dame, Ind.: Ave Maria Press, 1978.

Fox, Matthew. *The Coming of the Cosmic Christ*. New York: HarperCollins, 1988.

Girard, René. *The Scapegoat*. Baltimore, Md.: Johns Hopkins University Press, 1986.

Girard, René. *The Girard Reader*. Chestnut Ridge, N.Y.: Crossroad Publishing, 1996.

Gulley, Philip, and Mulholland, James. *If Grace Is True*. New York: HarperCollins, 2003.

Haidt, Jonathan. *The Happiness Hypothesis*. New York: Basic Books, 2006.

Hammerton-Kelly, Robert G. *Sacred Violence*. Minneapolis, Minn.: Augsburg Fortress Press, 1992.

Harvey, Andrew. *Teachings of the Christian Mystics*. Boston: Shambhala, 1998.

Heim, S. Mark. *Saved from Sacrifice: A Theology of the Cross*. Grand Rapids, Mich.: Wm. B. Eerdmans Publishing, 2006.

Kegan, Robert. *The Evolving Self*. Cambridge, Mass.: Harvard University Press, 1982.

Marion, Jim. *Putting on the Mind of Christ*. Charlottesville, Va.: Hampton Roads Publishing, 2000.

McFague, Sallie. *The Body of God*. Minneapolis, Minn.: Augsburg Fortress Press, 1993.

Meyendorff, John. *St. Gregory Palamas and Orthodox Spirituality*. Yonkers, N.Y.: St. Vladimir's Seminary Press, 1974.

Meyendorff, John, and Palamas, Gregory. *The Triads*. Mahwah, N.J.: Paulist Press, 1983.

Nancy, Jean-Luc. *Noli Me Tangere: On the Raising of the Body*. Bronx, N.Y.: Fordham University Press, 2008.

Nothwehr, Dawn M. *The Franciscan View of the Human Person: Some Central Elements*. St. Bonaventure, N.Y.: Franciscan Institute, St. Bonaventure University, 2003.

Ord, David Robert. *Your Forgotten Self*. Vancouver, B.C.: Namaste Printing, 2007.

Panikkar, Raimon. *Christophany: The Fullness of Man*. Maryknoll, N.Y.: Orbis Books, 2004.

Panikkar, Raimon. *The Experience of God: Icons of the Mystery*. Minneapolis, Minn.: Augsburg Fortress Press, 2006.

Perrin, Norman. *The Resurrection, According to Matthew, Mark and Luke*. Minneapolis, Minn.: Fortress Press, 1977.

Polkinghorne, John. *Science and the Trinity*. New Haven, Conn.: Yale University Press, 2004.

Robinson, John A. T. *In the End God*. New York: HarperCollins, 1968.

Sanford, John A. *Mystical Christianity*. Chestnut Ridge, N.Y.: Crossroad Publishing, 1993.

Sardello, Robert. *Silence: The Mystery of Wholeness*. Benson, N.C.: Goldenstone Press, 2006.

Savary, Louis M. *Teilhard de Chardin: The Divine Milieu, Explained*. Mahwah, N.J.: Paulist Press, 2007.

Singh, Kathleen Dowling. *The Grace in Dying*. New York: HarperCollins, 1998.

Smith, Huston. *Why Religion Matters*. New York: Harper-Collins, 2001.

Urs von Balthasar, Hans. *The Scandal of the Incarnation by St. Irenaeus*. San Francisco: Ignatius Press, 1990.

Vagaggini, Cipriano. *The Flesh: Instrument of Salvation*. Staten Island, N.Y.: Alba House, 1969.

Weaver, J. Denny. *The Nonviolent Atonement*. Grand Rapids, Mich.: Wm. B. Eerdmans, 2001.

Fr. Richard Rohr is a globally recognized ecumenical teacher bearing witness to the universal awakening within mystical and transformational traditions. A Franciscan priest of the New Mexico Province and founder of the Center for Action and Contemplation (CAC) in Albuquerque, New Mexico, his teaching is grounded in practices of contemplation and lived *kenosis* (self-emptying), expressing itself in radical compassion, particularly for the socially marginalized.

Fr. Richard is the author of numerous books, including *The Naked Now*, *Everything Belongs*, *Adam's Return*, *Breathing Under Water*, and *Falling Upward*.

CAC is home to the Rohr Institute and its Living School for Action and Contemplation. Fr. Richard is available to speak to groups convening in the New Mexico area. To learn more about the school, visit www.cac.org.

Center for Action and Contemplation

Home of THE ROHR INSTITUTE

The Center for Action and Contemplation was founded by Fr. Richard Rohr, OFM in 1987. Located in its original South Valley neighborhood in Albuquerque, New Mexico, it exemplifies the Franciscans' 800-year tradition of remaining visible and interactive in a highly populated and secular community.

The Center is home to the Rohr Institute which draws upon the Franciscan alternative orthodoxy, emphasizing practice over dogma. Its programs, including the Living School, bear witness to an ecumenical and inclusive Christianity grounded within its mystical traditions. The Center's education mission is to produce compassionate and powerfully learned individuals who will work for positive change in the world based on compassion for the suffering and an awareness of our common union with Divine Reality and all beings.

Are you ready to conspire for change?

Living School for
Action and Contemplation

Grounded in the Christian mystical tradition
Empowering individuals for compassionate action
Acknowledging our differences
Valuing our one-ness
That all may be one. –John 17:21
Learn more about the two-year program
and online courses at
www.cac.org

Falling Upward

A Spirituality for the Two Halves of Life

"Understanding the spiritual aspects of aging is as important as appreciating the systems and biological processes that age us. Richard Rohr has given us a perfect guide to what he calls the 'further journey,' a voyage into the mystery and beauty of healthy spiritual maturity."
—Mehmet Oz, M.D., host of the "Dr. Oz Show"

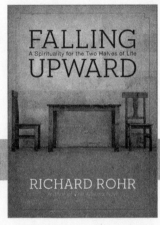

Hardcover | 240 p
$19.95 | 978-0-470-90775-7

In **_Falling Upward_**, Father Richard Rohr—the founder of the Center for Action and Contemplation—offers a new paradigm for understanding one of the most profound of life's mysteries: how our failings can be the foundation for our ongoing spiritual growth. Drawing on the wisdom from time-honored myths, heroic poems, great thinkers, and sacred religious texts, the author explores the two halves of life to show that those who have fallen, failed, or "gone down" are the only ones who understand "up." We grow spiritually more by doing it wrong than by doing it right.